Java Full Stack Interview Questions: Your Ultimate Preparation Guide

Author: Yash d.

While every precaution has been taken in the preparation of this book, the publisher assumes no responsibility for errors or omissions, or for damages resulting from the use of the information contained herein.

JAVA FULL STACK INTERVIEW QUESTIONS: YOUR ULTIMATE PREPARATION GUIDE

First edition. December 10, 2024.

Copyright © 2024 Yash d..

ISBN: 979-8227438140

Written by Yash d..

To all aspiring developers,who dare to dream and strive to achieve their goals in the ever-evolving world of technology. Your passion, curiosity, and determination inspire us every day. May this guide serve as a compass on your journey to mastering Java full-stack development and unlocking the door to countless opportunities.

To the mentors and educators,who dedicate their time and knowledge to guide the next generation of programmers. Your unwavering support and encouragement shape the future of our industry.

And to my family and friends,for your constant love, patience, and belief in my vision. Thank you for being my pillars of strength throughout this journey.

Here's to your success—may you conquer every interview and turn your aspirations into reality!

Preface

In today's fast-paced digital world, the demand for skilled Java Full Stack Developers continues to soar. Organizations seek professionals who can seamlessly navigate both front-end and back-end development, possessing a unique blend of technical knowledge, creativity, and problem-solving skills. This ebook, "Java Full Stack Interview Guide: A Step-by-Step Preparation Journey," aims to equip aspiring developers with the tools and strategies they need to excel in interviews and stand out in a competitive job market.

As you embark on this preparation journey, you will find a comprehensive roadmap that covers essential topics ranging from core Java concepts to advanced frameworks and database management. Each chapter is designed to build your understanding progressively, ensuring you grasp foundational principles before moving on to more complex subjects. We delve into the technical skills necessary for full stack development, while also addressing critical aspects such as behavioral interviews and negotiation tactics.

Recognizing the challenges candidates face when preparing for interviews, we have compiled a wealth of real-world interview questions and concise answers to help you familiarize yourself with the expectations of potential employers. Additionally, practical tips for managing anxiety, preparing effectively on the eve of your interview, and navigating salary discussions are included to enhance your confidence and readiness.

Whether you are a recent graduate entering the tech industry or an experienced professional looking to transition into a full stack role, this guide serves as your companion throughout the preparation process. By following the structured approach outlined in this ebook, you will develop a solid understanding of the skills required and gain the confidence to tackle interviews with ease.

We hope this guide inspires you to embark on your journey with enthusiasm and determination. The world of Java full stack development is vast and full of opportunities; with the right preparation, you can secure your dream role and contribute meaningfully to the field.

Best of luck in your interview preparation!

Chapter 1

Introduction to Java Full-Stack Development

What is Full Stack Development?

Full Stack Development refers to the comprehensive approach to web application development that encompasses both the front-end and back-end parts of a web application. The front-end is what users interact with directly—this includes everything from the layout and design of the website to the client-side scripting that makes the site dynamic and interactive. The back-end, on the other hand, is responsible for the server-side logic, database interactions, user authentication, and overall application performance.

A full stack developer possesses a diverse skill set that allows them to work on all aspects of a web application. They are familiar with various technologies, frameworks, and programming languages used in both front-end and back-end development. This versatility enables them to build an entire web application from scratch, troubleshoot issues across the stack, and collaborate more effectively with team members who specialize in specific areas.

The demand for full stack developers has surged in recent years due to the growing need for efficient and scalable web applications. Companies value developers who can understand both the client-side and server-side, allowing for smoother communication and faster project completion. This holistic understanding of the software development lifecycle is what sets full stack developers apart from their counterparts who specialize in only one area.

Why Java for Full Stack Development?

Java has established itself as one of the most popular programming languages for web development, and its suitability for full stack development is underscored by several compelling reasons:

1. Robustness and Stability

Java is known for its robustness, which comes from its strong memory management and exception-handling capabilities. This reliability is crucial in building large-scale enterprise applications that demand high uptime and performance. Businesses rely on Java to power mission-critical applications, and this stability extends to web development, making Java a preferred choice for full stack projects.

2. Platform Independence

One of Java's core strengths is its platform independence due to the Java Virtual Machine (JVM). Developers can write code once and run it anywhere, eliminating concerns about compatibility across different systems. This feature simplifies deployment and increases the reach of applications across various environments.

3. Extensive Ecosystem and Libraries

Java has a vast ecosystem that includes frameworks, libraries, and tools that facilitate rapid development. For the front end, Java developers often leverage frameworks like JavaServer Faces (JSF) or integrate Java with popular JavaScript frameworks such as Angular or React. For back-end development, Spring Boot has become a go-to framework for building microservices and RESTful APIs, providing a robust architecture for server-side applications.

4. Strong Community Support

Java boasts a large and active community of developers who contribute to its ongoing development and support. This means that developers can easily find resources, documentation, and forums to address any challenges they face. The availability of community-driven resources accelerates the learning curve for new developers and helps solve issues quickly.

5. Security Features

Security is paramount in web applications, especially those that handle sensitive data. Java provides a range of built-in security features, such as authentication, authorization, and encryption. The language also benefits from regular updates that address vulnerabilities, ensuring that applications built with Java can maintain high security standards.

6. Integration Capabilities

Java excels in integrating with other technologies, services, and databases. Full stack developers often need to connect their applications to various databases (both SQL and NoSQL), external APIs, and cloud services. Java's versatility allows it to seamlessly integrate with diverse technologies, making it an ideal choice for building full stack applications.

7. Career Opportunities

With the increasing demand for full stack developers proficient in Java, career opportunities in this field are abundant. Many organizations are looking for developers who can handle both front-end and back-end responsibilities, leading to higher job security and competitive salaries. The versatility gained from mastering full stack development with Java opens doors to various roles, including software engineer, application architect, and technical lead.

Key Skills and Technologies for a Java Full Stack Developer

To excel as a Java full stack developer, one must possess a diverse skill set that spans various technologies and methodologies. Here are the key skills and technologies that a Java full stack developer should focus on:

1. Proficiency in Core Java

Understanding the fundamentals of Java is crucial. This includes concepts such as object-oriented programming (OOP), data structures, algorithms, exception handling, and Java 8+ features like streams and lambdas. Mastery of these basics provides a strong foundation for building robust applications.

2. Frontend Technologies

A Java full stack developer should have a good grasp of front-end technologies, including:

- HTML/CSS: The building blocks of web design, essential for structuring and styling web pages.

- JavaScript: A key scripting language for adding interactivity to web applications.

- Frontend Frameworks: Familiarity with frameworks such as Angular, React, or Vue.js, which help streamline front-end development and improve user experience.

3. Backend Frameworks

A solid understanding of back-end frameworks is necessary for building the server-side of applications. Key frameworks include:

- Spring Framework: A powerful framework that simplifies Java application development. Spring Boot, in particular, is favored for its ease of use in creating microservices and RESTful APIs.

- Java Persistence API (JPA) / Hibernate: These are essential for handling database interactions and object-relational mapping.

4. Database Knowledge

Proficiency in both relational and NoSQL databases is crucial. Familiarity with SQL databases like MySQL or PostgreSQL, as well as NoSQL databases like MongoDB, enables developers to design effective data storage solutions.

5. RESTful API Development

Understanding how to create and consume RESTful APIs is essential for enabling communication between the front end and back end. Knowledge of API design principles, security, and documentation (e.g., using Swagger) is also beneficial.

6. Version Control with Git

Version control is vital for collaborative software development. Proficiency in Git allows developers to manage code changes effectively, collaborate with team members, and maintain a history of project revisions.

7. DevOps Practices

Familiarity with DevOps practices, including Continuous Integration (CI) and Continuous Deployment (CD), is increasingly important. Tools like Jenkins, Docker, and Kubernetes facilitate efficient deployment and scaling of applications.

8. Testing and Debugging Skills

A full stack developer should be proficient in writing tests (unit, integration, end-to-end) to ensure code quality. Familiarity with testing frameworks like JUnit and Mockito, along with debugging tools, is essential for maintaining reliable applications.

9. Soft Skills and Problem-Solving Abilities

While technical skills are paramount, soft skills such as communication, teamwork, and problem-solving are equally important. Full stack developers often collaborate with other team members, including designers and product managers, to bring applications to life. The ability to clearly articulate ideas, listen to feedback, and adapt to changing requirements is crucial for success in this role.

Interview Expectations: What Recruiters Look For

When it comes to interviewing candidates for full stack developer positions, recruiters generally focus on a combination of technical proficiency, problem-solving skills, and cultural fit. Here are some key aspects that recruiters typically evaluate:

1. Technical Knowledge

Candidates should demonstrate a strong understanding of Java and its associated frameworks. This includes knowledge of:

- Core Java concepts
- Spring and Hibernate for back-end development
- Front-end technologies such as HTML, CSS, and JavaScript
- Database management and SQL
- RESTful API design and implementation

Technical assessments may involve coding challenges, system design questions, or live coding sessions to gauge the candidate's ability to solve problems in real-time.

2. Practical Experience

Recruiters look for candidates with practical experience building full stack applications. This can include personal projects, internships, or professional experience. Being able to showcase a portfolio of work that demonstrates the candidate's skills in both front-end and back-end development is advantageous.

3. Problem-Solving Skills

Full stack developers must be adept problem solvers. Recruiters may present candidates with hypothetical scenarios or technical challenges during the interview to assess their analytical thinking and coding skills. The ability to approach problems methodically and arrive at effective solutions is a valuable trait.

4. Collaboration and Communication

Given the collaborative nature of software development, recruiters pay close attention to a candidate's communication skills. They often seek individuals who can articulate their thought processes clearly, collaborate effectively with team members, and adapt to feedback. Soft skills can significantly influence hiring decisions.

5. Cultural Fit

Finally, recruiters evaluate whether a candidate aligns with the company culture and values. This may involve assessing the candidate's work ethic, adaptability, and attitude towards learning. Cultural fit can play a crucial role in team dynamics and long-term job satisfaction.

In conclusion, understanding the fundamentals of full stack development, the advantages of using Java, and the key skills required can provide a strong foundation for aspiring developers. Preparing for interviews involves not only honing technical skills but also developing soft skills and practical experience that align with what recruiters are looking for. As the demand for Java full stack developers continues to grow, equipping yourself with the right knowledge and experience will enhance your prospects in this dynamic field.

Chapter 2
Core Java Fundamentals

OOP Concepts

1. What is Object-Oriented Programming (OOP)?

Answer: OOP is a programming paradigm based on the concept of "objects," which can contain data and methods. It promotes greater flexibility and maintainability in software design through key principles: encapsulation, inheritance, polymorphism, and abstraction.

2. Explain Inheritance in Java.

Answer: Inheritance is a mechanism where a new class (subclass) inherits attributes and methods from an existing class (superclass). This promotes code reusability. In Java, it is implemented using the `extends` keyword.

3. What is Polymorphism?

Answer: Polymorphism allows methods to perform differently based on the object that it is acting upon. It can be achieved through method overriding (runtime polymorphism) and method overloading (compile-time polymorphism).

4. What is Encapsulation?

Answer: Encapsulation is the technique of bundling the data (variables) and methods (functions) that operate on the data into a single unit (class). It restricts direct access to some of the object's components and can be achieved using access modifiers (private, public, protected).

5. Explain Abstraction with an example.

Answer: Abstraction is the concept of hiding complex implementation details and showing only the essential features of the object. In Java, it can be achieved using abstract classes and interfaces. For example, an abstract class `Shape` can define an abstract method `draw()`, which subclasses like `Circle` and `Rectangle` will implement.

Java Data Types, Collections, and Generics

6. What are the two types of data types in Java?

Answer: Java has two categories of data types:

1. Primitive Data Types: These include `int`, `char`, `double`, `boolean`, etc.

2. Reference Data Types: These refer to objects and include classes, interfaces, and arrays.

7. Explain the Java Collection Framework.

Answer: The Java Collection Framework is a set of classes and interfaces that implement commonly used data structures, such as lists, sets, and maps. It provides methods for manipulating collections of objects. Key interfaces include `List`, `Set`, and `Map`.

8. What is the difference between List and Set?

Answer:

- List: An ordered collection that allows duplicate elements. Examples include `ArrayList` and `LinkedList`.

- Set: A collection that does not allow duplicate elements. Examples include `HashSet` and `TreeSet`.

9. What are Generics in Java?

Answer: Generics enable types (classes and interfaces) to be parameters when defining classes, interfaces, and methods. This allows for stronger type checks at compile time and eliminates the need for casting. For example, `List<String>` is a generic list that can only hold `String` objects.

10. How do you create a generic method?

Answer: A generic method is defined with a type parameter. For example:

```java
public <T> void printArray(T[] array) {
for (T element : array) {
```

```
System.out.println(element);
    }
}
\ \ \
```

Exception Handling

11. What is Exception Handling in Java?

Answer: Exception handling is a mechanism to handle runtime errors, allowing the normal flow of the program to be maintained. It uses `try`, `catch`, `finally`, `throw`, and `throws` keywords.

12. What is the difference between checked and unchecked exceptions?

Answer:

- Checked Exceptions: These are checked at compile-time and must be either caught or declared in the method signature. Examples include `IOException` and `SQLException`.

- Unchecked Exceptions: These are not checked at compile-time. Examples include `NullPointerException` and `ArrayIndexOutOfBoundsException`.

13. Explain the try-catch-finally block.

Answer: The `try` block contains code that might throw an exception. The `catch` block handles the exception. The `finally` block always executes, regardless of whether an exception occurred, often used for cleanup code.

14. What is a custom exception?

Answer: A custom exception is a user-defined exception class that extends the `Exception` class. It allows developers to create meaningful error messages specific to their application.

Multithreading and Concurrency

15. What is multithreading in Java?

Answer: Multithreading is a concurrent execution of two or more threads, enabling parallel processing and better CPU utilization. In

Java, threads can be created by extending the `Thread` class or implementing the `Runnable` interface.

16. What is the difference between `Runnable` and `Thread`?

Answer:

- Runnable: An interface that represents a task that can be run by a thread. It must implement the `run()` method.

- Thread: A class that represents a thread of execution. It can either extend the `Thread` class or implement the `Runnable` interface.

17. What are the key methods in the Thread class?

Answer: Key methods include:

- `start()`: Starts the execution of the thread.

- `run()`: Contains the code to be executed by the thread.

- `sleep(long millis)`: Pauses the thread for a specified time.

- `join()`: Waits for the thread to die.

- `yield()`: Pauses the currently executing thread and allows others to execute.

18. What is synchronization in Java?

Answer: Synchronization is a mechanism to control access to shared resources by multiple threads. It prevents thread interference and ensures data consistency. It can be achieved using synchronized methods or blocks.

19. Explain the concept of a deadlock.

Answer: A deadlock occurs when two or more threads are blocked forever, waiting for each other to release resources. This situation typically arises when each thread holds a lock that the other thread needs.

Java 8+ Features

20. What are Lambda expressions in Java?

Answer: Lambda expressions are a way to implement functional interfaces (interfaces with a single abstract method) using an expression. They simplify the syntax for defining anonymous inner classes. For example:

```java
(x, y) -> x + y
```

21. Explain the Stream API in Java 8.

Answer: The Stream API allows processing sequences of elements (like collections) in a functional style. It supports operations like filtering, mapping, and reducing. Streams are lazy, meaning operations are not performed until a terminal operation is invoked.

22. What is the purpose of the `Optional` class?

Answer: The `Optional` class is a container object which may or may not contain a value. It is used to avoid `NullPointerExceptions` and to represent optional values more clearly. For example:

```java
Optional<String> name = Optional.ofNullable(getName());
```

23. What are functional interfaces?

Answer: A functional interface is an interface with a single abstract method. They can have multiple default or static methods. Functional interfaces are used primarily in lambda expressions. Examples include `Runnable`, `Callable`, and `Comparator`.

24. How do you use the `filter()` method in Streams?

Answer: The `filter()` method is used to select elements from a stream that match a given predicate. For example:

```java
List<String> names = Arrays.asList("Alice", "Bob", "Charlie");
List<String> filteredNames = names.stream()
.filter(name -> name.startsWith("A"))
.collect(Collectors.toList());
```

Key Interview Questions on Core Java

25. What is the difference between `==` and `equals()`?

Answer: `==` checks for reference equality (whether two references point to the same object), while `equals()` checks for value equality (whether two objects are logically equivalent).

26. What are the access modifiers in Java?

Answer: The four access modifiers in Java are:

- `private`: Accessible only within the same class.
- `default`: Accessible within the same package.
- `protected`: Accessible within the same package and subclasses.
- `public`: Accessible from any other class.

27. What is the significance of the `final` keyword?

Answer: The `final` keyword can be applied to classes, methods, and variables:

- Final Class: Cannot be subclassed.
- Final Method: Cannot be overridden.
- Final Variable: Its value cannot be changed once assigned.

28. What is the purpose of the `static` keyword?

Answer: The `static` keyword indicates that a member belongs to the class, rather than instances of the class. Static methods and variables can be accessed without creating an instance of the class.

29. How does garbage collection work in Java?

Answer: Garbage collection is the automatic process of reclaiming memory by deleting objects that are no longer reachable or referenced in the program. Java's garbage collector manages memory and runs periodically to free up memory.

30. What is the purpose of `this` keyword?

Answer: The `this` keyword refers to the current object instance. It is used to resolve ambiguity between instance variables and parameters, and it can also be used to call other constructors within the same class.

Chapter 3
Advanced Java Concepts

Java Memory Management and Garbage Collection

1. What is Java memory management?

Java memory management refers to the process of allocating and deallocating memory to Java objects. It is handled by the Java Virtual Machine (JVM), which includes automatic garbage collection to reclaim memory used by objects no longer in use.

2. Explain the Java heap and stack memory.

- Heap Memory: This is where Java objects are stored. The heap is shared among all threads and is managed by the garbage collector.

- Stack Memory: This memory is used for storing method frames, local variables, and references to objects in the heap. Each thread has its own stack.

3. What is garbage collection?

Garbage collection is the process of identifying and disposing of objects that are no longer reachable or needed by the program, thus freeing up memory.

4. Describe the types of garbage collectors in Java.

- Serial Garbage Collector: Uses a single thread for garbage collection. Best for small applications.

- Parallel Garbage Collector: Uses multiple threads to speed up garbage collection in applications with multiple processors.

- Concurrent Mark-Sweep (CMS) Collector: Performs garbage collection concurrently with the application threads to reduce pause times.

- G1 Garbage Collector: A server-style garbage collector that breaks the heap into regions and focuses on collecting the most garbage with minimal pause times.

5. How can you trigger garbage collection in Java?

You can suggest that the JVM performs garbage collection using `System.gc()`, but it is not guaranteed that the garbage collector will run immediately.

Java Design Patterns

6. What are design patterns in Java?

Design patterns are standard solutions to common software design problems. They provide a template for writing code that can be reused across various situations.

7. Explain the Singleton design pattern.

The Singleton pattern restricts the instantiation of a class to a single instance. This is useful when exactly one object is needed to coordinate actions.

Example Implementation:

```java
public class Singleton {
private static Singleton instance;
private Singleton() {}
public static Singleton getInstance() {
if (instance == null) {
instance = new Singleton();
}
return instance;
}
}
```

8. What is the Factory design pattern?

The Factory pattern provides an interface for creating objects but allows subclasses to alter the type of created objects. It promotes loose coupling by eliminating the need for the client to instantiate objects directly.

Example Implementation:
```java
interface Shape {
void draw();
}
class Circle implements Shape {
public void draw() {
System.out.println("Circle");
}
}
class Rectangle implements Shape {
public void draw() {
System.out.println("Rectangle");
}
}
class ShapeFactory {
public Shape getShape(String shapeType) {
if (shapeType.equalsIgnoreCase("CIRCLE")) {
return new Circle();
} else if (shapeType.equalsIgnoreCase("RECTANGLE")) {
return new Rectangle();
}
return null;
}
}
```

9. What is the Observer design pattern?

The Observer pattern defines a one-to-many dependency between objects so that when one object changes state, all its dependents are notified and updated automatically.

Example Implementation:
```java
```

```java
import java.util.ArrayList;
import java.util.List;
interface Observer {
void update(String message);
}
class Subject {
private List<Observer> observers = new ArrayList<>();
private String state;
public void attach(Observer observer) {
observers.add(observer);
}
public void setState(String state) {
this.state = state;
notifyAllObservers();
}
private void notifyAllObservers() {
for (Observer observer : observers) {
observer.update(state);
}
}
}
```

SOLID Principles in Java

10. What does SOLID stand for?
- S - Single Responsibility Principle
- O - Open/Closed Principle
- L - Liskov Substitution Principle
- I - Interface Segregation Principle
- D - Dependency Inversion Principle

11. Explain the Single Responsibility Principle (SRP).

A class should have only one reason to change, meaning it should have only one job or responsibility. This promotes cohesion.

12. What is the Open/Closed Principle (OCP)?

Software entities (classes, modules, functions, etc.) should be open for extension but closed for modification. This means you can add new functionality without altering existing code.

13. Define the Liskov Substitution Principle (LSP).

Objects of a superclass should be replaceable with objects of a subclass without affecting the correctness of the program. This ensures that derived classes extend the base classes without changing their behavior.

14. What is the Interface Segregation Principle (ISP)?

Clients should not be forced to depend on interfaces they do not use. This means that a class should implement only the methods that are relevant to it.

15. Explain the Dependency Inversion Principle (DIP).

High-level modules should not depend on low-level modules. Both should depend on abstractions. This promotes loose coupling and enhances code maintainability.

Working with Files and I/O

16. How do you read a file in Java?

You can use `BufferedReader` along with `FileReader` for reading text files.

Example:

```java
import java.io.;
public class FileReadExample {
public static void main(String[] args) throws IOException {
BufferedReader     br     =     new     BufferedReader(new FileReader("file.txt"));
```

```
String line;
while ((line = br.readLine()) != null) {
System.out.println(line);
}
br.close();
}
}
```

17. How do you write to a file in Java?

You can use `BufferedWriter` along with `FileWriter` to write text to files.

Example:
```java
import java.io.;
public class FileWriteExample {
public static void main(String[] args) throws IOException {
BufferedWriter      bw      =      new      BufferedWriter(new FileWriter("output.txt"));
bw.write("Hello, World!");
bw.close();
}
}
```

18. What is the difference between `InputStream` and `Reader`?

- InputStream: Used for reading byte data (e.g., images, binary files).

- Reader: Used for reading character data (e.g., text files). It supports Unicode.

Reflection and Annotations

19. What is reflection in Java?

Reflection is a feature that allows inspection and manipulation of classes, methods, and fields at runtime. It enables dynamic behavior, such as instantiating objects, invoking methods, and accessing fields.

20. How can you create an instance of a class using reflection?

You can use `Class.forName()` and `newInstance()` method.

Example:

```java
Class<?> cls = Class.forName("com.example.MyClass");
Object obj = cls.newInstance();
```

21. What are annotations in Java?

Annotations are metadata that provide information about the program but are not part of the program itself. They are used for various purposes, such as providing configuration or documentation.

22. How do you create a custom annotation?

You define an interface with the `@interface` keyword.

Example:

```java
import java.lang.annotation.;
@Retention(RetentionPolicy.RUNTIME)
@Target(ElementType.TYPE)
public @interface MyCustomAnnotation {
String value();
}
```

Concurrency and Synchronization in Java

23. What is concurrency in Java?

Concurrency is the ability to execute multiple threads simultaneously, allowing for more efficient use of resources and better application performance.

24. Explain the difference between `synchronized` method and `synchronized` block.

- Synchronized Method: Locks the entire method, which can lead to reduced performance if the method is long.

- Synchronized Block: Locks a specific block of code, providing more granular control and improving performance.

Example:

```java
public synchronized void syncMethod() {
// synchronized method code
}
public void method() {
synchronized(this) {
// synchronized block code
}
}
```

25. What is the `volatile` keyword in Java?

The `volatile` keyword is used to indicate that a variable's value will be modified by different threads. It ensures that updates to the variable are visible to all threads immediately, preventing caching issues.

26. What is a deadlock?

A deadlock occurs when two or more threads are blocked forever, waiting for each other to release resources. This can happen if two threads hold locks on different objects and each thread is trying to acquire the lock held by the other.

Advanced Interview Questions and Coding Challenges

27. What is the difference between `Callable` and `Runnable`?

- Runnable: Cannot return a result and cannot throw checked exceptions.

- Callable: Can return a result and can throw checked exceptions.

28. Describe the producer-consumer problem.

The producer-consumer problem is a classic synchronization problem where one or more producers generate data and put it into a buffer, while one or more consumers take data from the buffer. Proper synchronization is required to prevent data loss.

29. How do you handle thread safety in Java?

You can handle thread safety by using synchronization, concurrent collections (like `ConcurrentHashMap`), and avoiding shared mutable state.

30. What are the best practices for using threads in Java?

- Use higher-level concurrency utilities like `Executors`.

- Prefer immutable objects to avoid synchronization.

Chapter 4

Database Management and Persistence

SQL Basics

Q1: What are CRUD operations?

A1: CRUD stands for Create, Read, Update, and Delete, which are the four basic operations for managing data in a database.

Q2: How do you perform CRUD operations using SQL?

A2:

- Create: `INSERT INTO table_name (column1, column2) VALUES (value1, value2);`

- Read: `SELECT FROM table_name;`

- Update: `UPDATE table_name SET column1 = value1 WHERE condition;`

- Delete: `DELETE FROM table_name WHERE condition;`

Q3: What are SQL joins?

A3: SQL joins are used to combine records from two or more tables based on a related column. Types of joins include:

- INNER JOIN: Returns records with matching values in both tables.

- LEFT JOIN: Returns all records from the left table and matched records from the right table.

- RIGHT JOIN: Returns all records from the right table and matched records from the left table.

- FULL OUTER JOIN: Returns all records when there is a match in either left or right table records.

Q4: What is indexing in databases?

A4: Indexing is a data structure technique used to speed up the retrieval of rows from a database table. An index creates a pointer to the data, improving query performance at the cost of additional storage and slower write operations.

Q5: How do you create an index in SQL?

A5: You can create an index using the following SQL syntax:

```sql
CREATE INDEX index_name ON table_name (column_name);
```

Database Design and Normalization

Q6: What is database normalization?

A6: Normalization is the process of organizing a database to reduce redundancy and improve data integrity. It involves dividing large tables into smaller ones and defining relationships between them.

Q7: What are the different normal forms?

A7: The main normal forms are:

- First Normal Form (1NF): Ensures that all columns contain atomic values and each column is unique.

- Second Normal Form (2NF): Achieves 1NF and removes partial dependencies on a composite primary key.

- Third Normal Form (3NF): Achieves 2NF and removes transitive dependencies.

Q8: Can you explain the concept of foreign keys?

A8: A foreign key is a column or a set of columns in one table that refers to the primary key in another table, establishing a relationship between the two tables.

Introduction to NoSQL

Q9: What is NoSQL?

A9: NoSQL refers to a class of database management systems that do not use SQL as their primary interface. They are designed for specific types of data models and provide flexible schema designs, scalability, and high performance.

Q10: What are the main types of NoSQL databases?

A10: The main types include:

- Document Stores (e.g., MongoDB): Store data as documents (JSON-like format).

- Key-Value Stores (e.g., Redis): Store data as key-value pairs.

- Column Family Stores (e.g., Cassandra): Store data in columns rather than rows.

- Graph Databases (e.g., Neo4j): Store data as nodes and relationships for complex queries.

Q11: What are the benefits of using MongoDB?

A11: MongoDB offers schema flexibility, horizontal scalability, rich query capabilities, built-in sharding, and the ability to handle large volumes of unstructured data.

Q12: How does Cassandra achieve high availability?

A12: Cassandra achieves high availability through its decentralized architecture, replication across multiple nodes, and eventual consistency model, ensuring no single point of failure.

ORM with Hibernate/JPA

Q13: What is ORM?

A13: Object-Relational Mapping (ORM) is a programming technique that converts data between incompatible type systems using object-oriented programming languages.

Q14: What are Hibernate and JPA?

A14: Hibernate is a popular ORM framework for Java, while JPA (Java Persistence API) is a specification that provides a standard for ORM in Java. Hibernate implements the JPA specification.

Q15: How do you map a Java class to a database table in Hibernate?

A15: You can use annotations like `@Entity` for the class, `@Table` for the table name, and `@Id` for the primary key. Example:

```java
@Entity
@Table(name = "users")
public class User {
@Id
@GeneratedValue(strategy = GenerationType.IDENTITY)
private Long id;
```

```
@Column(name = "username")
private String username;
}
```

Q16: What are relationships in Hibernate?

A16: Relationships define how two entities interact. Types include:

- One-to-One: One entity relates to one instance of another entity.

- One-to-Many: One entity relates to multiple instances of another entity.

- Many-to-Many: Multiple instances of one entity relate to multiple instances of another entity.

Q17: What is caching in Hibernate?

A17: Caching in Hibernate is a mechanism to store frequently accessed data in memory to reduce database access. It includes:

- First-Level Cache: Session-specific, enabled by default.

- Second-Level Cache: Shared across sessions, requires configuration.

Transactions and ACID Properties

Q18: What is a database transaction?

A18: A database transaction is a sequence of operations performed as a single logical unit of work, which must be completed in its entirety or not at all.

Q19: What are the ACID properties?

A19: ACID stands for:

- Atomicity: Transactions are all-or-nothing.

- Consistency: Transactions must leave the database in a valid state.

- Isolation: Transactions should not affect each other until completed.

- Durability: Once a transaction is committed, it remains so, even in the event of a system failure.

Q20: How do you handle transactions in Hibernate?

A20: You handle transactions in Hibernate using `Transaction` objects:

```java
Session session = sessionFactory.openSession();
Transaction transaction = session.beginTransaction();
try {
// Perform operations
transaction.commit();
} catch (Exception e) {
transaction.rollback();
} finally {
session.close();
}
```

Common Interview Questions on Databases and Persistence

Q21: How do you optimize database queries?

A21: You can optimize database queries by:

- Using indexes appropriately.

- Avoiding SELECT ; instead, select only required columns.

- Writing efficient JOINs and avoiding unnecessary ones.

- Using WHERE clauses to filter records early.

Q22: What is the difference between SQL and NoSQL?

A22: SQL databases are relational and use structured query language with predefined schemas, while NoSQL databases are non-relational, offer flexible schemas, and are better suited for unstructured or semi-structured data.

Q23: What are the trade-offs of using NoSQL databases?

A23: NoSQL databases provide scalability and flexibility but may lack ACID compliance, which can lead to data consistency challenges.

Q24: How would you choose between SQL and NoSQL for a project?

A24: Choose SQL for structured data with complex relationships and transactions. Opt for NoSQL when handling unstructured data, requiring high scalability and flexibility.

Q25: What is denormalization and when would you use it?

A25: Denormalization is the process of intentionally introducing redundancy into a database schema to improve read performance. It's used when read performance is prioritized over write efficiency, such as in data warehousing.

Q26: Explain the concept of a database index and its types.

A26: A database index is a data structure that improves the speed of data retrieval operations. Types include:

- B-tree Indexes: Balanced tree structure, commonly used.

- Hash Indexes: Uses a hash table for equality searches.

- Full-text Indexes: Used for searching text within string columns.

Q27: What are transactions in SQL, and how do you implement them?

A27: Transactions in SQL group multiple operations into a single unit. You can implement them using the `BEGIN`, `COMMIT`, and `ROLLBACK` statements to control the transaction lifecycle.

Q28: What is a view in SQL?

A28: A view is a virtual table based on the result of a SELECT query. It can simplify complex queries and enhance security by restricting access to specific data.

Q29: What is the purpose of a stored procedure?

A29: A stored procedure is a set of precompiled SQL statements stored in the database. It promotes code reuse, improves performance, and allows for better security through encapsulation of business logic.

Q30: How do you ensure data integrity in a database?

A30: Data integrity is ensured through:

- Primary and foreign keys.

- Constraints (e.g., UNIQUE, NOT NULL).

- Transactions with ACID properties.

Chapter 5

Backend Development with Spring Framework

Introduction to Spring Framework: Why It's Important

The Spring Framework is a powerful and flexible framework for building enterprise applications in Java. It promotes good design practices through its support for loose coupling, high cohesion, and dependency injection. The Spring ecosystem provides a variety of tools to create robust applications, making it essential for modern Java development.

Spring Core: Dependency Injection, Bean Lifecycle

Q1: What is Dependency Injection (DI)?

A: Dependency Injection is a design pattern that allows the creation of loosely coupled applications. In Spring, DI enables the framework to manage object creation and injection of dependencies at runtime, which simplifies testing and promotes separation of concerns.

Q2: How do you define a Spring Bean?

A: A Spring Bean is an object that is instantiated, configured, and managed by the Spring IoC (Inversion of Control) container. Beans are typically defined in XML files or annotated with annotations like `@Component`, `@Service`, `@Repository`, and `@Controller`.

Q3: What is the Bean Lifecycle in Spring?

A: The Bean Lifecycle consists of several phases:

1. Instantiation: The Spring container instantiates the bean.

2. Populate Properties: The container sets the properties using DI.

3. Set Bean Name: The bean's name is set if applicable.

4. Set Bean Factory: The container provides the BeanFactory.

5. Post-Process Before Initialization: Custom initialization logic can be applied.

6. Initialization: The bean is initialized, possibly with a custom method.

7. Post-Process After Initialization: Additional post-processing can occur.

8. Destruction: The bean is destroyed when the container is closed or when the bean is no longer needed.

Q4: Explain the difference between `@Component`, `@Service`, `@Repository`, and `@Controller`.

A:

- `@Component`: A generic stereotype for any Spring-managed component.

- `@Service`: Indicates that a class performs service tasks, typically containing business logic.

- `@Repository`: Specifies that a class is a Data Access Object (DAO), encapsulating the logic to access data sources.

- `@Controller`: Marks a class as a Spring MVC controller that handles HTTP requests.

Spring Boot: Microservices, Application Setup, Configurations

Q5: What is Spring Boot and its advantages?

A: Spring Boot is an extension of the Spring framework that simplifies the setup and development of new applications. Advantages include:

- Convention over configuration: Reduces the need for boilerplate code.

- Embedded server support: No need for external web servers (e.g., Tomcat).

- Easy dependency management with Spring Initializr.

- Production-ready features like health checks and metrics.

Q6: How do you create a Spring Boot application?

A: A Spring Boot application can be created using Spring Initializr (https://start.spring.io/) by selecting the necessary dependencies and generating a project. You can also use the command line or IDE tools (e.g., IntelliJ IDEA) to bootstrap the application.

Q7: What is the purpose of `application.properties` or `application.yml` in Spring Boot?

A: The `application.properties` or `application.yml` file is used for external configuration of the Spring Boot application. It allows developers to define application settings such as server port, database configurations, logging levels, and custom application properties.

Q8: Explain the concept of microservices in Spring Boot.

A: Microservices architecture involves developing applications as a suite of small, independent services, each running in its process and communicating via lightweight mechanisms (usually HTTP). Spring Boot facilitates microservices development by providing tools for service discovery, API gateway, and circuit breakers, among other features.

Spring Data: Working with Databases (JPA, Spring Data MongoDB)

Q9: What is Spring Data?

A: Spring Data is a part of the Spring framework that simplifies data access and manipulation in applications. It provides support for various data stores, including relational databases (via JPA) and NoSQL databases (like MongoDB).

Q10: Explain the purpose of JPA in Spring Data.

A: JPA (Java Persistence API) is a specification for accessing, persisting, and managing data between Java objects and relational databases. Spring Data JPA simplifies the implementation of JPA-based data access layers by providing a set of repositories and methods to perform CRUD operations.

Q11: How do you create a repository interface in Spring Data JPA?

A: You create a repository interface by extending `JpaRepository` or `CrudRepository`. For example:

```java
public interface UserRepository extends JpaRepository<User, Long> {
List<User> findByLastName(String lastName);
}
```

Q12: How does Spring Data MongoDB differ from JPA?

A: Spring Data MongoDB is designed for NoSQL database interaction and uses BSON instead of SQL. While JPA relies on relational database concepts like tables and joins, MongoDB works with collections and documents, focusing on unstructured data.

Spring MVC: Handling HTTP Requests, REST API Development

Q13: What is Spring MVC?

A: Spring MVC (Model-View-Controller) is a web framework within the Spring framework that provides a way to build web applications following the MVC design pattern. It allows for the separation of concerns, making it easier to manage application complexity.

Q14: How do you define a RESTful web service in Spring MVC?

A: A RESTful web service in Spring MVC can be defined using the `@RestController` annotation. For example:

```java
@RestController
@RequestMapping("/api/users")
public class UserController {
@GetMapping("/{id}")
public User getUser(@PathVariable Long id) {
return userService.findById(id);
}
}
```

Q15: Explain the role of `@RequestMapping`, `@GetMapping`, and `@PostMapping`.

A:

- `@RequestMapping`: Used to map web requests to specific handler methods or classes.

- `@GetMapping`: A specialized version of `@RequestMapping` for handling HTTP GET requests.

- `@PostMapping`: A specialized version of `@RequestMapping` for handling HTTP POST requests.

Q16: What is the purpose of `@PathVariable` and `@RequestParam`?
   A:
   - `@PathVariable`: Used to extract values from the URI path. For example, in `/users/{id}`, `id` can be accessed with `@PathVariable("id")`.
   - `@RequestParam`: Used to extract query parameters from the URL. For example, in `/users?age=25`, the age can be accessed with `@RequestParam("age")`.

Spring Security: Authentication, Authorization, JWT
   Q17: What is Spring Security?
   A: Spring Security is a powerful authentication and access-control framework for Java applications. It provides comprehensive security services for Java EE-based enterprise software applications.

Q18: Explain the difference between authentication and authorization.
   A:
   - Authentication: The process of verifying the identity of a user or system.
   - Authorization: The process of granting or denying access to specific resources or actions based on the authenticated user's permissions.

Q19: How do you secure a Spring Boot application with Spring Security?

A: You can secure a Spring Boot application by adding Spring Security as a dependency, configuring security settings in a `@Configuration` class, and using `@EnableWebSecurity`. You define access rules using the `HttpSecurity` object in the `configure()` method.

Q20: What is JWT, and how is it used in Spring Security?

A: JWT (JSON Web Token) is an open standard for securely transmitting information between parties as a JSON object. In Spring Security, JWT is used for stateless authentication, allowing users to authenticate once and receive a token for subsequent requests without needing to log in again.

Q21: Describe the basic flow of JWT authentication.

A: The flow of JWT authentication is as follows:

1. The user logs in with credentials (username and password).

2. The server verifies the credentials and generates a JWT.

3. The server sends the JWT to the client, which stores it (typically in local storage).

4. For subsequent requests, the client sends the JWT in the `Authorization` header.

5. The server verifies the token and grants access to protected resources.

Common Backend Interview Questions

Q22: What is the difference between @Component and @Service?

A: `@Component` is a general-purpose stereotype for any Spring-managed component, while `@Service` specifically denotes a service layer component, typically containing business logic. Using `@Service` enhances clarity about the class's purpose.

Q23: Explain how to handle exceptions globally in a Spring Boot application.

A: You can handle exceptions globally using the `@ControllerAdvice` annotation. This allows you to define a class that can catch exceptions thrown by any controller and return a custom response.

Chapter 6
Frontend Development: JavaScript, HTML, and CSS

HTML5 and CSS3: Key Concepts and Best Practices

1. What is HTML5?

- HTML5 is the latest version of Hypertext Markup Language that provides better support for multimedia and enhances web applications with features like new semantic elements, form controls, and local storage.

2. What are semantic elements in HTML5?

- Semantic elements clearly describe their meaning in a human- and machine-readable way, e.g., `<header>`, `<footer>`, `<article>`, and `<section>`, improving accessibility and SEO.

3. What is the purpose of the `<canvas>` element in HTML5?

- The `<canvas>` element allows for dynamic, scriptable rendering of 2D shapes and bitmap images, making it ideal for games, animations, and graphical applications.

4. What are web forms in HTML5, and what are some new input types?

- HTML5 introduced new input types like `email`, `url`, `tel`, `date`, and `range`, which enhance user experience by providing built-in validation and specific user interfaces.

5. What is CSS3?

- CSS3 is the latest version of Cascading Style Sheets, introducing new features such as media queries, transitions, animations, and flexbox for responsive design.

6. What are media queries in CSS3?

- Media queries allow for the application of CSS styles based on the device characteristics like screen size, resolution, and orientation, enabling responsive design.

7. What are CSS Flexbox and Grid?

- Flexbox is a one-dimensional layout model that allows items to align and distribute space within a container. Grid is a two-dimensional layout model that enables complex layouts with rows and columns.

8. How can you optimize CSS for performance?

- Minimize CSS file sizes, combine multiple CSS files, use CSS preprocessors (like SASS/LESS), remove unused styles, and utilize shorthand properties to optimize performance.

9. What is the box model in CSS?

- The box model describes the rectangular boxes generated for elements in the document tree, including margins, borders, padding, and the actual content area.

10. How do you implement responsive design using CSS?

- Use flexible grid layouts, set max-widths instead of fixed widths, apply media queries to adjust styles based on screen size, and leverage CSS frameworks like Bootstrap.

JavaScript Fundamentals: ES6+ Features

11. What is JavaScript?

- JavaScript is a high-level, dynamic, and interpreted programming language that enables interactive web pages. It is an essential part of web development alongside HTML and CSS.

12. What are let, const, and var?

- `var` declares variables with function scope, `let` declares block-scoped variables, and `const` declares block-scoped variables that cannot be reassigned.

13. What is a JavaScript arrow function?

- Arrow functions provide a more concise syntax for writing function expressions and lexically bind the `this` value, allowing easier access to the surrounding scope.

14. What are template literals in JavaScript?

- Template literals are string literals that allow embedded expressions, multi-line strings, and easier string formatting using backticks (``) instead of quotes.

15. What is destructuring assignment?

- Destructuring assignment is a syntax that allows unpacking values from arrays or properties from objects into distinct variables.

16. What are Promises in JavaScript?

- Promises are objects that represent the eventual completion (or failure) of an asynchronous operation and its resulting value, enabling easier management of asynchronous code.

17. What is the spread operator?

- The spread operator (`...`) allows an iterable (like an array) to be expanded in places where zero or more elements are expected, useful for copying and merging arrays or objects.

18. What is an IIFE (Immediately Invoked Function Expression)?

- An IIFE is a JavaScript function that runs as soon as it is defined, providing a way to create a private scope and avoid polluting the global namespace.

19. What are JavaScript modules?

- Modules are reusable pieces of code that can be exported from one file and imported into another, promoting better organization and separation of concerns in JavaScript applications.

20. What is async/await?

- `async/await` is syntactic sugar built on top of Promises, making it easier to work with asynchronous code by allowing asynchronous functions to be written in a synchronous style.

DOM Manipulation, Events, and AJAX

21. What is the DOM?

- The Document Object Model (DOM) is a programming interface for web documents that represents the page structure as a tree of objects, allowing languages like JavaScript to manipulate HTML and CSS.

22. How do you select an element in the DOM?

- Use methods like `document.getElementById()`, `document.querySelector()`, and `document.getElementsByClassName()` to select elements in the DOM.

23. What is event delegation?

- Event delegation is a technique that involves using a single event listener on a parent element to manage events for multiple child elements, improving performance and simplifying code.

24. How do you handle events in JavaScript?

- Events can be handled using methods like `addEventListener()` for attaching event listeners to elements, and event objects are passed to the handler functions.

25. What is AJAX?

- Asynchronous JavaScript and XML (AJAX) is a technique for making asynchronous requests to a server without reloading the entire page, enhancing user experience.

26. How can you make an AJAX request?

- Use the `XMLHttpRequest` object or the `fetch()` API to make AJAX requests to retrieve data from a server asynchronously.

27. What is JSON?

- JSON (JavaScript Object Notation) is a lightweight data interchange format that is easy for humans to read and write, and easy for machines to parse and generate.

28. What are callback functions in JavaScript?

- Callback functions are functions passed as arguments to other functions, allowing asynchronous behavior by being executed after a certain event or completion of a task.

29. What is the difference between `fetch` and `XMLHttpRequest`?

- The `fetch` API is a modern interface that returns Promises and has a more powerful and flexible feature set, while `XMLHttpRequest` is older, callback-based, and less convenient for handling requests.

30. How do you handle errors in AJAX calls?

- Handle errors using `try...catch` blocks with async/await or by using `.catch()` with Promises to catch and respond to errors that may occur during the request.

Responsive Design with CSS Frameworks (Bootstrap, Material UI)

31. What is responsive design?

- Responsive design is an approach that makes web pages render well on a variety of devices and window or screen sizes, ensuring a good user experience across all devices.

32. What is Bootstrap?

- Bootstrap is a popular front-end framework that provides CSS and JavaScript components for building responsive and mobile-first web applications quickly and efficiently.

33. What are Bootstrap grid system classes?

- Bootstrap's grid system uses a series of containers, rows, and columns to layout and align content, with classes like `.container`, `.row`, and `.col-` to define structure.

34. How do you customize Bootstrap styles?

- Customize Bootstrap styles by overriding default styles in your CSS file, using Sass variables, or utilizing the Bootstrap customization tool to create a tailored version of Bootstrap.

35. What is Material UI?

- Material UI is a popular React component library that implements Google's Material Design principles, providing pre-styled components for building user interfaces quickly.

36. What are the advantages of using CSS frameworks?

- CSS frameworks offer pre-designed components, responsive grid systems, faster development, consistent design, and built-in support for accessibility.

37. What is the difference between fixed, fluid, and responsive layouts?

- Fixed layouts have a set width, fluid layouts expand to fill the container's width, and responsive layouts adapt to different screen sizes using media queries.

38. What is a breakpoint in responsive design?

- A breakpoint is a specific screen width where the layout of the webpage changes to accommodate different devices, typically defined using media queries.

39. How can you create a responsive image?

- Use CSS properties like `max-width: 100%;` and `height: auto;` to ensure images scale with their containing element without losing aspect ratio.

40. What are the best practices for responsive design?

- Use relative units (like percentages), implement fluid grids, utilize media queries, optimize images for different resolutions, and test across various devices and browsers.

Client-Side Interview Questions and Scenarios

41. How do you optimize front-end performance?

- Optimize performance by minimizing HTTP requests, compressing files, using lazy loading, implementing caching strategies, and optimizing images.

42. What is CORS?

- Cross-Origin Resource Sharing (CORS) is a security feature that allows or restricts resources on a web page to be requested from another domain outside the domain from which the first resource was served.

43. What are single-page applications (SPAs)?

- SPAs are web applications that load a single HTML page and dynamically update the content as the user interacts with the app, resulting in a smoother user experience.

Chapter 7

Frontend Frameworks: Angular or React

Introduction to Single-Page Applications (SPA)

Q1: What is a Single-Page Application (SPA)?

A: An SPA is a web application that interacts with the user by dynamically rewriting the current page, rather than loading entire new pages from the server. This leads to a more fluid user experience.

Q2: What are the advantages of SPAs?

A: SPAs offer faster load times, improved user experience, and seamless navigation. They reduce server load since only data is sent over the network instead of complete HTML pages.

Q3: What are some common examples of SPAs?

A: Examples include Gmail, Google Maps, and Trello.

Core Concepts of Angular

Q4: What are Angular Modules?

A: Angular Modules (NgModules) are containers for a cohesive block of code dedicated to an application domain, workflow, or closely related set of capabilities. Each Angular application has at least one root module.

Q5: What is a Component in Angular?

A: A Component is a building block of Angular applications. It controls a patch of screen called a view and contains the logic to manage the view and handle user interactions.

Q6: What are Services in Angular?

A: Services are singleton objects that are instantiated only once during the lifetime of an application. They are used to encapsulate business logic, data access, and share functionality across components.

Q7: What are Directives in Angular?

A: Directives are classes that add additional behavior to elements in Angular applications. There are three types: Components, Structural Directives (like `ngFor` and `ngIf`), and Attribute Directives (like `ngStyle`).

Core Concepts of React

Q8: What is JSX in React?

A: JSX is a syntax extension for JavaScript that looks similar to XML or HTML. It allows developers to write HTML structures in the same file as JavaScript code, which makes the code easier to read and write.

Q9: What are Components in React?

A: Components are reusable UI elements that can manage their state and props. They can be functional (using hooks) or class-based, and they return React elements to describe what should appear on the screen.

Q10: What are Props in React?

A: Props (short for properties) are read-only attributes that are passed from parent components to child components. They allow data to be passed down the component tree.

Q11: What is State in React?

A: State is a built-in object that allows components to create and manage their own dynamic data. Unlike props, state can be modified within the component.

Q12: What are Hooks in React?

A: Hooks are functions that let you use state and other React features in functional components. Common hooks include `useState`, `useEffect`, and `useContext`.

Data Binding and Event Handling

Q13: What is data binding in Angular?

A: Data binding is the mechanism that establishes a connection between the application UI and the underlying data model. Angular supports two-way data binding, allowing both the view and model to be updated simultaneously.

Q14: How does event handling work in Angular?

A: In Angular, event handling is done using Angular templates. You can listen for events using the `(eventName)` syntax, e.g., `(click)="onClick()"`.

Q15: What is data binding in React?

A: Data binding in React is unidirectional. Data flows from parent components to child components via props, and to update the state, functions are used to handle events.

Q16: How do you handle events in React?

A: In React, events are handled using camelCase syntax. You can define event handler functions and pass them as props, e.g., `<button onClick={this.handleClick}>Click Me</button>`.

Working with APIs: Fetching Data with HTTP

Q17: How do you fetch data from an API in Angular?

A: In Angular, you can use the `HttpClient` module to perform HTTP requests. You can inject `HttpClient` in a service and use methods like `get()`, `post()`, etc., to fetch or send data.

Q18: What is the purpose of Observables in Angular?

A: Observables are a part of RxJS and are used to handle asynchronous data streams. They provide powerful capabilities for managing data, such as composing multiple data streams and reacting to data changes.

Q19: How do you fetch data in React?

A: In React, you typically use the `fetch` API or libraries like `Axios` to retrieve data from an API. This can be done in lifecycle methods or using the `useEffect` hook in functional components.

Q20: What is the use of async/await in API calls?

A: The `async/await` syntax simplifies asynchronous code. It allows you to write asynchronous code that looks synchronous, making it easier to read and understand.

Routing and State Management

Q21: What is routing in Angular?

A: Routing in Angular allows you to navigate between different views or components within a single-page application. It is handled by the Angular Router, which manages the application's routes.

Q22: How do you implement routing in Angular?

A: You define routes in the `RouterModule` and configure them with path and component pairs. Use `<router-outlet>` to display the routed components in the template.

Q23: What is state management in React?

A: State management refers to how data is handled across components in a React application. It can be managed locally within components or globally using tools like Redux or the Context API.

Q24: What is Redux?

A: Redux is a predictable state container for JavaScript applications. It allows you to manage the state globally with a single store and ensures that the state can only be changed via actions and reducers.

Q25: How does the Context API work in React?

A: The Context API allows you to share values (like state) between components without having to explicitly pass props through every level of the component tree. You create a context and use `Provider` to supply the value.

Frontend Frameworks Interview Questions

Q26: What are the differences between Angular and React?

A: Angular is a full-fledged MVC framework while React is a library focused on building UI components. Angular uses TypeScript and has a more opinionated structure, whereas React offers more flexibility with JavaScript and component-based architecture.

Q27: Can you explain the component lifecycle in React?

A: React components have a lifecycle that can be divided into three phases: Mounting (initialization), Updating (when props/state change), and Unmounting (cleanup). Key lifecycle methods include `componentDidMount`, `componentDidUpdate`, and `componentWillUnmount`.

Q28: What are Angular Lifecycle Hooks?

A: Angular lifecycle hooks are methods that allow you to tap into key events in a component's lifecycle. Key hooks include `ngOnInit`, `ngOnChanges`, `ngOnDestroy`, etc.

Q29: What is two-way data binding?

A: Two-way data binding allows changes in the UI to reflect in the model and vice versa. It is commonly used in Angular, where the `[(ngModel)]` directive enables two-way data binding.

Q30: What is one advantage of using React Hooks?

A: One advantage of using React Hooks is that they allow you to manage state and side effects in functional components, making it easier to share logic between components without using higher-order components or render props.

Q31: How do you manage forms in Angular?

A: Angular provides reactive and template-driven forms for managing user input. Reactive forms are more scalable and offer more control, while template-driven forms are simpler and use two-way data binding.

Q32: What is lazy loading in Angular?

A: Lazy loading is a design pattern used to load components or modules only when they are needed, which improves the application's initial load time. It is configured in the Angular router.

Q33: How do you optimize performance in React?

A: Performance in React can be optimized by using React.memo to prevent unnecessary re-renders, using the `useCallback` and `useMemo` hooks, and employing code splitting to load only necessary components.

Q34: What is a higher-order component (HOC) in React?

A: A higher-order component is a function that takes a component and returns a new component, enabling you to reuse component logic. HOCs are commonly used for cross-cutting concerns like authentication and data fetching.

Q35: How do you handle errors in Angular applications?

A: In Angular, errors can be handled globally using the `ErrorHandler` class or locally using try/catch blocks in services or components. Additionally, HTTP interceptors can be used for handling API errors.

This overview provides a structured approach to important topics in Angular and React, focusing on essential interview questions and concise answers. You can expand on these points as needed to reach your word count or include practical examples and code snippets for clarification.

Chapter 8
Building RESTful APIs

RESTful Web Services: Key Concepts and Principles

1. What is REST?

- Answer: REST (Representational State Transfer) is an architectural style for designing networked applications that rely on stateless, client-server communication using standard HTTP methods.

2. What are the key principles of REST?

- Answer:

- Statelessness: Each request from a client contains all the information the server needs to fulfill that request.

- Client-Server Architecture: Separation of client and server allows them to evolve independently.

- Cacheability: Responses must define themselves as cacheable or not to improve performance.

- Uniform Interface: A standard way to interact with resources using HTTP methods (GET, POST, PUT, DELETE).

- Layered System: The architecture can be composed of layers, allowing for scalability and flexibility.

3. What are resources in REST?

- Answer: Resources are any piece of information that can be accessed or manipulated via the API, identified by URIs (Uniform Resource Identifiers).

4. What are the common HTTP methods used in RESTful APIs?

- Answer: The common methods include:

- GET: Retrieve data.

- POST: Create a new resource.

- PUT: Update an existing resource.

- DELETE: Remove a resource.

5. What is a URI, and why is it important?

- Answer: A URI (Uniform Resource Identifier) uniquely identifies a resource. It is crucial for accessing and manipulating resources in a RESTful API.

Designing RESTful APIs: Best Practices

6. What are some best practices for designing RESTful APIs?

- Answer:

- Use meaningful and descriptive resource names.

- Use nouns for resource URIs (e.g., `/users`, `/orders`).

- Implement proper status codes (200 for success, 404 for not found, etc.).

- Support filtering, sorting, and pagination in responses.

- Version the API to manage changes effectively (e.g., `/v1/users`).

- Return data in a consistent format, usually JSON or XML.

7. How should you handle errors in a RESTful API?

- Answer: Use standard HTTP status codes and return a structured error response that includes an error message, code, and any relevant details.

8. What is HATEOAS, and how does it relate to REST?

- Answer: HATEOAS (Hypermedia as the Engine of Application State) is a constraint of REST that allows clients to interact with the API entirely through hypermedia links provided in responses, reducing coupling between the client and server.

9. How can you ensure your API is versioned?

- Answer: Include the version number in the URI or use custom headers. For example, `/v1/users` or `Accept: application/vnd.yourapi.v1+json`.

10. What role do status codes play in RESTful APIs?

- Answer: Status codes inform clients about the outcome of their requests, allowing them to handle responses appropriately. Common codes include:

- 200 OK: Request succeeded.

- 201 Created: Resource successfully created.

- 400 Bad Request: Invalid request syntax.
- 401 Unauthorized: Authentication required.
- 500 Internal Server Error: Server error occurred.

Securing APIs with Authentication and Authorization

11. What are the common authentication methods for RESTful APIs?

- Answer: Common methods include:
- Basic Authentication: Transmits credentials as base64 encoded strings.
- Token-Based Authentication: Clients receive a token after logging in, which is used for subsequent requests.
- OAuth 2.0: A more secure method that allows third-party applications to access user data without exposing credentials.

12. What is the difference between authentication and authorization?

- Answer: Authentication verifies who a user is (e.g., logging in), while authorization determines what an authenticated user can do (e.g., permissions for accessing resources).

13. How can you secure a RESTful API?

- Answer:
- Implement HTTPS to encrypt data in transit.
- Use authentication mechanisms (e.g., OAuth, JWT).
- Validate and sanitize inputs to prevent attacks like SQL injection.
- Rate limit API requests to prevent abuse.
- Regularly update dependencies to patch vulnerabilities.

14. What is JSON Web Token (JWT), and how is it used?

- Answer: JWT is a compact, URL-safe means of representing claims to be transferred between two parties. It is often used for authentication by passing a signed token in the header of API requests.

15. How can CORS (Cross-Origin Resource Sharing) be managed in REST APIs?

- Answer: CORS can be managed by setting appropriate HTTP headers (e.g., `Access-Control-Allow-Origin`) on the server to specify which domains are allowed to access the API.

Swagger for API Documentation

16. What is Swagger, and why is it used?

- Answer: Swagger (now known as OpenAPI Specification) is a framework for API documentation that allows developers to describe the API structure and operations, enabling easier consumption and integration.

17. How do you create API documentation using Swagger?

- Answer: By using annotations in your code (for example, in Spring), you can define endpoints, request parameters, responses, and descriptions that Swagger can parse to generate interactive documentation.

18. What are the benefits of using Swagger for API documentation?

- Answer:

- Provides an interactive UI for testing endpoints.

- Facilitates better communication between teams and stakeholders.

- Automatically generates client SDKs in various languages.

- Encourages consistent API design and documentation practices.

19. How can you version your Swagger documentation?

- Answer: By maintaining different API specifications for each version (e.g., `/v1/api-docs`, `/v2/api-docs`) and allowing users to switch between them in the documentation UI.

20. What is the purpose of Swagger UI?

- Answer: Swagger UI is a web-based interface that allows users to visualize and interact with the API's endpoints, making it easier to understand how to use the API and test it in real-time.

Key Questions on API Design and Development

21. What are some common pitfalls in API design?

- Answer: Common pitfalls include:
- Poorly defined resource names and URIs.
- Overly complex endpoints.
- Inconsistent response formats.
- Lack of versioning and documentation.

22. How would you handle rate limiting in an API?

- Answer: Rate limiting can be handled by tracking the number of requests from a client over a defined period and responding with a `429 Too Many Requests` status if the limit is exceeded.

23. What is the importance of API testing?

- Answer: API testing ensures that the API behaves as expected, performs well under load, and handles error scenarios gracefully, ultimately improving reliability and user experience.

24. How can you optimize the performance of a RESTful API?

- Answer: Performance can be optimized by:
- Implementing caching (both server-side and client-side).
- Minimizing data transfer by sending only required fields (using projections).
- Reducing the number of requests through batch processing.
- Using compression (e.g., Gzip) for responses.

25. How do you handle backward compatibility in API versions?

- Answer: To maintain backward compatibility, ensure that older versions of the API remain functional while new versions introduce enhancements. This can be done by not removing or changing existing endpoints and providing clear documentation on deprecated features.

26. What tools do you use for API testing?

- Answer: Common tools for API testing include Postman, Insomnia, SoapUI, and automated testing frameworks like JUnit or TestNG for integration tests.

27. How do you ensure the security of sensitive data in API responses?

- Answer: Sensitive data should be encrypted during transit using HTTPS, and it should not be included in API responses unless absolutely necessary. Use tokenization and data masking techniques where applicable.

28. What is API Gateway, and why is it used?

- Answer: An API Gateway acts as a single entry point for all client requests to a microservices architecture, providing functionalities such as load balancing, caching, security, and request routing.

29. How do you document error responses in your API?

- Answer: Document error responses by providing a standard format in the API documentation that includes status codes, error messages, and possible solutions or next steps for users.

30. Why is it important to follow RESTful principles?

- Answer: Following RESTful principles leads to cleaner, more maintainable APIs, enhances interoperability between systems, and provides a better experience for developers who consume the API.

This structured approach focuses on essential concepts and practical knowledge required for building RESTful APIs, ensuring readers have a solid foundation for interview preparation.

Sure! Here's a detailed yet concise exploration of Microservices Architecture, including definitions, benefits, challenges, and relevant interview questions with short answers.

Chapter 9
Microservices Architecture

What are Microservices?

Definition:

Microservices are an architectural style that structures an application as a collection of small, loosely coupled, independently deployable services. Each service focuses on a specific business capability and can be developed, deployed, and scaled independently.

Benefits:

- Scalability: Each microservice can be scaled independently based on demand.

- Flexibility: Different technologies and programming languages can be used for different services.

- Resilience: Failure in one service does not necessarily bring down the entire system.

- Faster Time to Market: Teams can work on different services simultaneously, speeding up development and deployment.

- Easier Maintenance: Smaller codebases make services easier to understand and maintain.

Challenges:

- Complexity: Managing multiple services can be complicated in terms of deployment and monitoring.

- Data Management: Handling data consistency across services can be challenging.

- Network Latency: Increased network calls between services can lead to latency issues.

- Security: Each service must be secured individually, increasing the attack surface.

- Operational Overhead: Requires more infrastructure and monitoring tools.

Spring Boot for Microservices

Definition:

Spring Boot is an open-source framework that simplifies the development of new applications based on the Spring framework. It provides a range of features for microservices, including embedded servers, automatic configuration, and production-ready features.

Key Features:

- Auto Configuration: Simplifies the setup of microservices by automatically configuring Spring components based on the dependencies.

- Embedded Servers: Supports embedded web servers like Tomcat and Jetty, making it easy to deploy microservices.

- Actuator: Provides built-in endpoints for monitoring and managing the application.

- Spring Cloud Integration: Offers tools for developing cloud-native microservices.

Service Discovery with Eureka

Definition:

Eureka is a service discovery tool that helps in locating services for the purpose of load balancing and failover of middle-tier servers. It is a REST-based service that is part of the Spring Cloud Netflix project.

Key Concepts:

- Client-side Discovery: Services register themselves with Eureka, and clients can look up services via the Eureka server.

- Load Balancing: Eureka helps distribute client requests to different instances of a service.

- Health Checks: Eureka performs health checks on registered services to ensure they are available for requests.

API Gateway with Zuul or Spring Cloud Gateway

Definition:

An API Gateway is a server that acts as an entry point for all client requests to a microservices architecture. It can route requests to the appropriate service and aggregate responses.

Zuul Features:

- Dynamic Routing: Routes requests to different services based on rules defined in the configuration.

- Load Balancing: Can be integrated with Eureka to perform client-side load balancing.

- Security: Centralized authentication and authorization can be implemented at the gateway level.

Spring Cloud Gateway Features:

- WebFlux Support: Built on Project Reactor, it supports reactive programming.

- Easy Configuration: Provides a simpler API for routing and filtering requests.

- Integration with Spring Security: Enables easier security management for APIs.

Inter-Service Communication (RestTemplate, Feign Client)

Inter-Service Communication:

Microservices communicate with each other using RESTful APIs, message queues, or event streams.

RestTemplate:

- A synchronous client to make HTTP requests in Spring applications.

- Commonly used for calling REST services from one microservice to another.

- Example usage:

```java
RestTemplate restTemplate = new RestTemplate();
String response = restTemplate.getForObject("http://service-url/api/resource", String.class);
```

Feign Client:
- A declarative web service client for easier integration with RESTful services.
- Reduces boilerplate code by allowing you to create an interface for the service.
- Example usage:
```java
@FeignClient(name = "service-name")
public interface ServiceClient {
@GetMapping("/api/resource")
String getResource();
}
```

Distributed Tracing and Monitoring (Zipkin, Sleuth)

Distributed Tracing:

In a microservices architecture, tracing requests through multiple services helps identify performance bottlenecks and errors.

Zipkin:
- A distributed tracing system that collects timing data for requests across microservices.
- Provides visualization of the call flow, helping to identify latencies.

Spring Cloud Sleuth:
- Integrates with Spring applications to add tracing capabilities.

- Automatically instruments the application and propagates trace information in HTTP headers.

- Works seamlessly with Zipkin for visualizing traces.

Microservices Interview Questions

1. What are microservices?

- Microservices are an architectural style that structures applications as a collection of small, independently deployable services.

2. What are the advantages of microservices?

- Scalability, flexibility in technology choices, resilience, faster time to market, and easier maintenance.

3. What challenges do microservices pose?

- Complexity in management, data consistency, network latency, security concerns, and operational overhead.

4. How does Spring Boot facilitate microservices development?

- Spring Boot offers auto-configuration, embedded servers, and easy integration with Spring Cloud for microservices.

5. What is Eureka, and why is it important?

- Eureka is a service discovery tool that allows services to find and communicate with each other, enabling load balancing and failover.

6. What is the role of an API Gateway?

- An API Gateway acts as a single entry point for clients to access multiple services, handling routing, load balancing, and security.

7. What is the difference between RestTemplate and Feign Client?

- RestTemplate is a synchronous client for making HTTP requests, while Feign Client is a declarative web service client that simplifies REST service calls.

8. What is distributed tracing, and why is it important?

- Distributed tracing tracks requests across multiple services, helping to identify bottlenecks and troubleshoot issues in a microservices architecture.

9. How do you implement monitoring in microservices?

- Monitoring can be implemented using tools like Zipkin for tracing and Spring Boot Actuator for application metrics.

10. What are some best practices for microservices architecture?

- Use a decentralized data management approach, implement API versioning, apply the single responsibility principle, and ensure service resilience with circuit breakers.

11. What is the purpose of Spring Cloud?

- Spring Cloud provides tools and frameworks to facilitate the development of cloud-native applications, including service discovery, configuration management, and routing.

12. What are circuit breakers, and why are they used?

- Circuit breakers prevent a service from trying to execute an operation that is likely to fail, enhancing system resilience by stopping repeated failures.

13. Can you explain service orchestration vs. service choreography?

- Service orchestration centralizes the control of interactions through a single service, while choreography allows services to communicate with each other directly without a central coordinator.

14. What is the significance of API versioning in microservices?

- API versioning allows backward compatibility when changes are made, ensuring that existing clients continue to function without interruption.

15. How do you handle data consistency in microservices?

- Implement patterns like Event Sourcing or Saga for managing data consistency across distributed services.

This structured overview of Microservices Architecture, with relevant questions and answers, serves as a comprehensive guide for interview preparation while highlighting essential concepts in the microservices domain.

Chapter 10
Version Control with Git and CI/CD Pipelines

Git Basics: Branching, Merging, Pull Requests

1. What is Git?

- Git is a distributed version control system used to track changes in source code during software development.

2. What is a branch in Git?

- A branch is a lightweight, movable pointer to a commit, allowing developers to work on features, fixes, or experiments independently from the main codebase.

3. How do you create a new branch in Git?

- Use the command: `git checkout -b branch-name`

4. What is merging in Git?

- Merging is the process of combining changes from one branch into another. The most common merge is from a feature branch back to the main branch.

5. What is a Pull Request (PR)?

- A Pull Request is a request to merge changes from one branch into another, typically used in collaborative workflows to review code before merging.

6. How do you resolve merge conflicts?

- Identify the conflicting files, edit them to resolve conflicts manually, and then use `git add` to stage the changes and `git commit` to finalize the merge.

7. What is the difference between `git merge` and `git rebase`?

- `git merge` creates a new commit that combines the changes, preserving history, while `git rebase` rewrites the commit history to create a linear progression.

8. What is a remote repository in Git?

- A remote repository is a version of your project that is hosted on the internet or a network, allowing collaboration with other developers.

9. How do you push changes to a remote repository?

- Use the command: `git push origin branch-name`

10. What does `git pull` do?

- `git pull` fetches changes from a remote repository and merges them into the current branch.

Continuous Integration/Continuous Deployment (CI/CD) Overview

11. What is CI/CD?

- CI/CD stands for Continuous Integration and Continuous Deployment, a set of practices that automate the integration and deployment of code changes.

12. What is Continuous Integration (CI)?

- CI is the practice of automatically testing and integrating code changes into a shared repository frequently, ensuring code quality and reducing integration issues.

13. What is Continuous Deployment (CD)?

- CD is the practice of automatically deploying all code changes to production after they pass testing, allowing for faster and more reliable releases.

14. What are the benefits of CI/CD?

- Benefits include faster release cycles, improved code quality, reduced integration issues, and increased collaboration among team members.

15. What tools are commonly used for CI/CD?

- Popular CI/CD tools include Jenkins, GitLab CI/CD, Travis CI, CircleCI, and Azure DevOps.

16. What is a CI/CD pipeline?

- A CI/CD pipeline is an automated workflow that facilitates the process of building, testing, and deploying applications.

Setting Up Jenkins or GitLab CI/CD

17. What is Jenkins?

- Jenkins is an open-source automation server used to implement CI/CD by enabling developers to build, test, and deploy their code.

18. How do you set up a Jenkins job?

- Create a new job in Jenkins, specify the repository URL, configure build triggers, and define build steps (like running scripts or commands).

19. What is a Jenkins pipeline?

- A Jenkins pipeline is a set of plugins that support implementing and integrating continuous delivery pipelines into Jenkins.

20. What is GitLab CI/CD?

- GitLab CI/CD is a built-in feature of GitLab that provides a robust system for continuous integration and deployment directly integrated with the version control system.

21. How do you configure a GitLab CI/CD pipeline?

- Define a `.gitlab-ci.yml` file in the root of your repository, specifying stages, jobs, and scripts for building, testing, and deploying your application.

22. What is a build trigger in CI/CD?

- A build trigger is an event that automatically starts a build process, such as pushing code to a repository or creating a merge request.

23. What are environment variables in CI/CD?

- Environment variables are dynamic values that can affect the behavior of scripts or processes in CI/CD pipelines, often used for configuration settings.

Automated Testing and Code Quality Tools (JUnit, SonarQube)

24. What is automated testing?

- Automated testing involves using software tools to run tests on the code automatically, ensuring its functionality and reliability without manual intervention.

25. What is JUnit?

- JUnit is a popular Java testing framework that allows developers to write and run repeatable tests to ensure the correctness of their code.

26. How do you write a simple JUnit test?

- Use annotations like `@Test`, and within the test method, assert expected outcomes using assertions like `assertEquals()`.

27. What is code coverage?

- Code coverage measures the percentage of code that is executed during testing, indicating the effectiveness of the test suite.

28. What is SonarQube?

- SonarQube is an open-source platform for continuous inspection of code quality, providing metrics, issues, and code reviews.

29. What are some key metrics provided by SonarQube?

- Key metrics include code coverage, duplications, code smells, bugs, vulnerabilities, and maintainability ratings.

30. How can you integrate JUnit with CI/CD?

- Configure CI/CD pipelines to automatically run JUnit tests during build processes to ensure code quality and functionality.

Docker and Kubernetes Overview

31. What is Docker?

- Docker is a platform that enables developers to automate the deployment of applications within lightweight containers.

32. What is a Docker container?

- A Docker container is a standardized unit of software packaging that includes the application code, libraries, dependencies, and runtime.

33. What is a Docker image?

- A Docker image is a read-only template used to create containers. It contains the application and all its dependencies.

34. How do you create a Docker image?

- Create a `Dockerfile` with instructions on how to build the image, then use the command: `docker build -t image-name .`

35. What is Kubernetes?

- Kubernetes is an open-source container orchestration platform that automates the deployment, scaling, and management of containerized applications.

36. What is a Pod in Kubernetes?

- A Pod is the smallest deployable unit in Kubernetes, representing a single instance of a running process in your cluster.

37. How do you scale a deployment in Kubernetes?

- Use the command: `kubectl scale deployment deployment-name—replicas=n` to change the number of replicas.

38. What is a Kubernetes Service?

- A Service in Kubernetes is an abstraction that defines a logical set of Pods and a policy to access them, often used for load balancing.

39. What are Helm charts?

- Helm charts are packages of pre-configured Kubernetes resources that facilitate the deployment and management of applications in Kubernetes clusters.

40. How do you deploy a Docker container to Kubernetes?

- Use a Deployment YAML file to define the desired state and deploy it using the command: `kubectl apply -f deployment.yaml`.

DevOps Integration Questions in Full Stack Interviews

41. What is DevOps?

- DevOps is a set of practices that combine software development (Dev) and IT operations (Ops) to shorten the development lifecycle and deliver high-quality software.

42. How does DevOps benefit software development?

- DevOps promotes collaboration, increases deployment frequency, improves recovery times, and ensures more stable operating environments.

43. What is Infrastructure as Code (IaC)?

- IaC is the practice of managing and provisioning computing infrastructure through machine-readable configuration files rather than physical hardware configuration.

44. What tools are commonly used in DevOps?

- Common tools include Docker, Kubernetes, Jenkins, Git, Terraform, Ansible, and monitoring tools like Prometheus and Grafana.

45. What is the role of automation in DevOps?

- Automation is essential in DevOps for tasks like testing, building, deployment, and monitoring, leading to faster and more reliable software delivery.

46. How do you monitor application performance in a CI/CD pipeline?

- Use monitoring tools (like New Relic, Prometheus, or Grafana) to track application performance and metrics post-deployment.

47. What is a rollback in CI/CD?

- A rollback is a process of reverting to a previous stable version of an application after a failed deployment or issue.

48. How do you ensure security in a CI/CD pipeline?

- Implement security measures such as automated security testing, static code analysis, and secret management throughout the pipeline.

49. What is a canary deployment?

- A canary deployment is a strategy where a new version of an application is rolled out to a small subset of users before a full deployment to monitor for issues.

50. What is the importance of version control in DevOps?

- Version control is crucial in DevOps for tracking changes, collaborating on code, and maintaining a history of the development process.

This compilation of questions and short answers is designed to cover essential topics

Chapter 11
Testing Your Application

Unit Testing in Java (JUnit, Mockito)

Q1: What is unit testing?

A1: Unit testing is a software testing method where individual components of a program (units) are tested in isolation to ensure they work as intended.

Q2: What is JUnit?

A2: JUnit is a widely-used testing framework for Java that provides annotations to identify test methods, assert statements to verify expected results, and test runners to execute tests.

Q3: How do you create a basic JUnit test case?

A3: A basic JUnit test case is created by defining a class annotated with `@Test`, implementing methods with assertions. Example:

```java
import org.junit.jupiter.api.Test;
import static org.junit.jupiter.api.Assertions.assertEquals;
public class CalculatorTest {
@Test
public void testAdd() {
Calculator calc = new Calculator();
assertEquals(5, calc.add(2, 3));
}
}
```

Q4: What are Mockito and its main features?

A4: Mockito is a mocking framework for Java that allows you to create mock objects for unit testing. Main features include creating mock objects, verifying interactions, and stubbing methods.

Q5: How do you create a mock object using Mockito?

A5: You create a mock object using the `mock()` method. Example:

```java
import static org.mockito.Mockito.;
public class MyServiceTest {
@Test
public void testService() {
MyService service = mock(MyService.class);
when(service.someMethod()).thenReturn("Mocked Response");
}
}
```

Q6: What are some best practices for unit testing?

A6: Best practices include:
- Write tests before code (TDD).
- Keep tests independent.
- Use descriptive names for test cases.
- Test only one behavior per test.
- Clean up after tests using `@AfterEach`.

Integration Testing with Spring

Q7: What is integration testing?

A7: Integration testing verifies that different components of the application work together as expected, often involving multiple modules, services, and databases.

Q8: How do you perform integration testing in Spring?

A8: Integration testing in Spring can be done using `@SpringBootTest`, which loads the full application context. Example:

```java
import org.springframework.boot.test.context.SpringBootTest;
@SpringBootTest
public class ApplicationIntegrationTest {
// Test methods go here
}
```

Q9: What is the purpose of the `@Autowired` annotation in integration tests?

A9: The `@Autowired` annotation allows Spring to automatically inject the required beans into the test class, enabling access to application components during testing.

Q10: How can you test REST APIs in Spring integration tests?

A10: REST APIs can be tested using `TestRestTemplate` or `MockMvc`. Example with `MockMvc`:

```java
```

```java
import                                                    static
org.springframework.test.web.servlet.request.MockMvcRequestBuilders.g
import                                                    static
org.springframework.test.web.servlet.result.MockMvcResultMatchers.stat
@Test
public void testGetEndpoint() throws Exception {
mockMvc.perform(get("/api/resource"))
.andExpect(status().isOk());
}
```

Q11: What is the difference between unit testing and integration testing?

A11: Unit testing focuses on individual components in isolation, while integration testing evaluates the interactions and collaboration between multiple components in the application.

Q12: What are some common challenges in integration testing?
A12: Challenges include:
- Dependency management and configuration issues.
- Environment setup and data management.
- Handling timeouts and race conditions.
- Maintaining test data consistency.

End-to-End Testing: Tools and Frameworks (Selenium, Cypress)
Q13: What is end-to-end testing?
A13: End-to-end testing is a testing method that validates the entire application flow from start to finish, ensuring all components work together as intended in a production-like environment.

Q14: What is Selenium?

A14: Selenium is an open-source testing framework for automating web applications for testing purposes. It supports multiple browsers and programming languages.

Q15: How do you create a simple Selenium test?

A15: A simple Selenium test involves initializing the WebDriver, navigating to a URL, and interacting with web elements. Example:

```java
import org.openqa.selenium.WebDriver;
import org.openqa.selenium.chrome.ChromeDriver;
public class SeleniumTest {
public static void main(String[] args) {
WebDriver driver = new ChromeDriver();
driver.get("http://example.com");
// Additional interactions
driver.quit();
}
}
```

Q16: What is Cypress?

A16: Cypress is a modern end-to-end testing framework designed for web applications, offering features like time travel, automatic waiting, and easy setup.

Q17: How does Cypress differ from Selenium?

A17: Cypress runs directly in the browser, providing better debugging and easier setup. It does not require a WebDriver and supports time travel and automatic waiting, while Selenium requires additional configuration.

Q18: What is the Cypress test structure?

A18: Cypress tests are structured using Mocha syntax, with `describe()` blocks for test suites and `it()` blocks for individual tests. Example:

```javascript
describe('My First Test', () => {
it('Visits the Kitchen Sink', () => {
cy.visit('http://example.com');
cy.get('h1').should('contain', 'Kitchen Sink');
});
});
```

Q19: What are some best practices for end-to-end testing?

A19: Best practices include:
- Keep tests independent and idempotent.
- Avoid using real APIs; use mocks or stubs.
- Regularly maintain and refactor test code.
- Run end-to-end tests in a CI/CD pipeline.

Writing Effective Test Cases for Full Stack Applications

Q20: What makes a good test case?

A20: A good test case is clear, concise, and covers a specific functionality. It includes preconditions, input data, execution steps, and expected results.

Q21: How do you write effective unit test cases?

A21: Effective unit test cases should:

- Test a single functionality.
- Use descriptive names.
- Cover edge cases and error scenarios.
- Assert the correct output for various inputs.

Q22: What should you include in integration test cases?

A22: Integration test cases should include:

- Setup and teardown methods for the application context.
- Valid and invalid input scenarios.
- Assertions on response status, body, and headers.
- Testing inter-service communication.

Q23: What is the importance of test coverage?

A23: Test coverage measures the percentage of code tested by unit tests. High test coverage helps ensure that most code paths are exercised, reducing the likelihood of undetected bugs.

Q24: How do you handle flaky tests?

A24: Flaky tests can be addressed by:

- Investigating and fixing underlying issues.
- Isolating tests to avoid shared state.
- Using retries for non-deterministic tests.

- Avoiding reliance on external services.

Testing Strategy Questions in Interviews

Q25: What is a testing strategy?

A25: A testing strategy outlines the overall approach to testing in a project, including types of testing, tools used, scope, resources, and timelines.

Q26: How do you choose the right testing tools for a project?

A26: The right tools are chosen based on:
- Project requirements (technology stack, team expertise).
- Type of testing (unit, integration, end-to-end).
- Community support and documentation.
- Integration capabilities with CI/CD pipelines.

Q27: What is the role of automated testing in a full stack application?

A27: Automated testing increases efficiency by running tests quickly and repeatedly, ensures consistent test execution, and allows for rapid feedback during development.

Q28: How do you prioritize test cases?

A28: Test cases are prioritized based on:
- Business impact and risk assessment.
- Frequency of use.
- Complexity of the functionality.
- Historical defect rates.

Q29: What are some common metrics used to evaluate testing effectiveness?

A29: Common metrics include:

- Test coverage percentage.

- Number of test cases executed.

- Pass/fail rate of tests.

- Time taken to run tests.

- Defect density.

Q30: Can you explain the concept of "shift-left" testing?

A30: Shift-left testing emphasizes testing earlier in the software development lifecycle (SDLC) to identify defects sooner, reduce costs, and improve product quality by integrating testing activities from the start of development.

This chapter provides a concise overview of critical topics related to testing in Java Full Stack applications, incorporating essential interview questions and their short answers.

Chapter 12
Debugging, Optimization, and Code Refactoring

Debugging Techniques in Java (IDE Tools, Logs)

1. What are common debugging tools used in Java?

Answer: Common debugging tools in Java include:

- Integrated Development Environment (IDE) Debuggers: Eclipse, IntelliJ IDEA, and NetBeans offer built-in debuggers for setting breakpoints, stepping through code, and inspecting variable states.

- Logging Frameworks: Log4j, SLF4J, and Java Util Logging help log application behavior for troubleshooting without stopping execution.

2. How do you set a breakpoint in an IDE?

Answer: In most IDEs, you can set a breakpoint by clicking in the margin next to the line number where you want the execution to pause. This allows you to inspect the current state and variable values.

3. What is the purpose of logging in debugging?

Answer: Logging provides insights into application flow, errors, and performance metrics. It helps track the application's behavior over time and is invaluable for diagnosing issues in production environments.

4. How do you read stack traces in Java?

Answer: A stack trace lists method calls leading to an exception. The top of the stack shows the method where the exception occurred, followed by the methods that called it. Analyzing the stack helps identify where and why an error happened.

5. What are the advantages of using a debugger over print statements?

Answer: A debugger allows interactive code execution, setting breakpoints, inspecting variables, and evaluating expressions in real time, making it more efficient and less intrusive than using print statements.

Performance Optimization Strategies

6. What are some common performance bottlenecks in Java applications?

Answer: Common bottlenecks include:

- Inefficient algorithms and data structures
- Excessive object creation and garbage collection
- Network latency in distributed applications
- Database access and query inefficiencies

7. How can you improve the performance of a Java application?

Answer: You can improve performance by:

- Optimizing algorithms and data structures
- Reducing object creation, using object pools
- Using caching mechanisms to minimize database calls
- Leveraging multithreading for parallel processing

8. What is lazy loading, and how does it improve performance?

Answer: Lazy loading defers the initialization of an object until it is needed, reducing startup time and memory usage, which can improve overall application performance.

9. How do you analyze performance issues in a Java application?

Answer: Analyze performance issues using profiling tools to identify bottlenecks, monitor resource usage, and examine thread behavior. Tools like VisualVM and JProfiler can help visualize performance metrics.

10. What is garbage collection, and how can it impact performance?

Answer: Garbage collection automatically manages memory by reclaiming objects that are no longer in use. However, frequent or inefficient garbage collection can lead to performance degradation due to pause times.

Profiling Tools and Memory Leak Detection

11. What is a Java profiler?

Answer: A Java profiler is a tool that measures the performance of Java applications, providing insights into memory usage, CPU load, and thread activity. It helps identify bottlenecks and areas for optimization.

12. How do you detect memory leaks in Java?

Answer: Memory leaks can be detected using profiling tools such as Eclipse Memory Analyzer (MAT) or VisualVM, which analyze heap dumps to find objects that are not being released and their reference paths.

13. What are the signs of a memory leak?

Answer: Signs of memory leaks include increased memory usage over time, frequent garbage collection cycles, and `OutOfMemoryError` exceptions indicating that the heap space is exhausted.

14. Explain how to use JConsole for monitoring Java applications.

Answer: JConsole is a monitoring tool that connects to Java applications via JMX (Java Management Extensions). It displays performance metrics such as memory usage, thread activity, and CPU load in real time, helping identify performance issues.

15. What is a heap dump, and how is it used?

Answer: A heap dump is a snapshot of the memory used by a Java application at a particular time. It is used for analyzing memory usage, identifying memory leaks, and understanding object retention patterns.

Code Refactoring Best Practices

16. What is code refactoring?

Answer: Code refactoring is the process of restructuring existing code without changing its external behavior to improve readability, reduce complexity, and enhance maintainability.

17. Why is code refactoring important?

Answer: Refactoring helps to keep the codebase clean, understandable, and adaptable to changes. It reduces technical debt and enhances the overall quality of the software.

18. What are common refactoring techniques?

Answer: Common refactoring techniques include:

- Extract Method: Breaking large methods into smaller, more manageable ones.

- Rename Variable: Using meaningful names to improve readability.

- Introduce Parameter Object: Grouping related parameters into a single object.

- Replace Magic Numbers: Using constants instead of hard-coded values for clarity.

19. When should you refactor code?

Answer: Refactoring should be considered when:

- Code becomes difficult to understand or maintain.

- There are recurring patterns or duplications.

- New features are added that require modifications to existing code.

20. How do you ensure refactoring does not introduce bugs?

Answer: To ensure that refactoring does not introduce bugs:

- Write unit tests before refactoring to cover existing functionality.

- Refactor in small increments and test frequently.

- Use automated tests to verify that the behavior remains unchanged.

Coding Standards and Clean Code

21. What are coding standards?

Answer: Coding standards are a set of guidelines and best practices for writing code. They ensure consistency, readability, and maintainability across the codebase, making it easier for teams to collaborate.

22. What are some key principles of clean code?

Answer: Key principles of clean code include:

- Meaningful Naming: Use descriptive names for variables, methods, and classes.

- Single Responsibility Principle: Each class or method should have one reason to change.

- Avoid Code Duplication: Reuse code through abstraction and modularization.

- Commenting and Documentation: Use comments judiciously to clarify complex logic, but avoid unnecessary comments.

23. How do you handle code reviews to maintain coding standards?

Answer: Handle code reviews by establishing clear guidelines, encouraging constructive feedback, and using automated tools (like SonarQube) to check for adherence to coding standards.

24. What tools can help enforce coding standards in Java?

Answer: Tools like Checkstyle, PMD, and SonarQube can help enforce coding standards by analyzing code for compliance with best practices and identifying potential issues.

25. How do you balance performance and readability in code?

Answer: Balance performance and readability by writing clean, understandable code first. If performance issues arise, identify bottlenecks and optimize those specific areas while maintaining overall readability.

Problem-Solving Questions on Optimization and Refactoring

26. How would you approach optimizing a slow-running method?

Answer: To optimize a slow-running method:

1. Use a profiler to identify performance bottlenecks.

2. Analyze the algorithm's complexity (Big O notation).

3. Optimize data structures and reduce unnecessary computations.

4. Consider caching frequently accessed data.

5. Refactor the code for better readability and maintainability.

27. Describe a situation where you had to refactor a large codebase. What steps did you take?

Answer: In refactoring a large codebase:

1. Conducted a thorough code review to identify areas for improvement.

2. Prioritized high-impact sections and wrote unit tests to cover existing functionality.

3. Applied refactoring techniques incrementally and continuously tested after each change.

4. Documented changes and communicated with the team to ensure understanding.

28. How do you decide whether to optimize code or leave it as is?

Answer: Decide to optimize based on:

- The frequency of the code being executed.

- Whether it impacts user experience significantly.

- The complexity introduced by optimization.

If it's a critical path or performance-intensive section, optimization may be warranted.

29. What strategies would you use to reduce the memory footprint of a Java application?

Answer: To reduce memory footprint:

1. Use primitive data types instead of wrapper classes where possible.

2. Limit the scope of variables and release resources when not needed.

3. Employ lazy initialization and avoid unnecessary object creation.

4. Use appropriate collections (e.g., `ArrayList` vs. `LinkedList`) based on access patterns.

30. How do you approach troubleshooting a performance issue in a production environment?

Answer: Approach troubleshooting by:

1. Gathering logs and metrics to identify the affected components.

2. Analyzing performance data using profiling tools.

3. Reproducing the issue in a development or staging environment if possible.

4. Implementing targeted fixes while monitoring the impact on performance.

This chapter provides a comprehensive set of interview questions and answers focusing on debugging, optimization, and code refactoring practices, which are essential skills for a Java full-stack developer. Each question encourages a deeper understanding of the principles and practices that contribute to high-quality software development.

Chapter 13
System Design and Architecture

This section is structured to cover the key topics you mentioned: system design basics, database design and sharding, caching mechanisms, API rate limiting, and throttling.

System Design Basics

1. What is scaling, and what are the two types?

Answer: Scaling refers to increasing the capacity of a system to handle a growing amount of work. The two types are:

- Vertical Scaling (Scaling Up): Adding more resources (CPU, RAM) to a single server.

- Horizontal Scaling (Scaling Out): Adding more machines or servers to distribute the load.

2. What is load balancing?

Answer: Load balancing is the process of distributing network traffic across multiple servers to ensure no single server becomes overwhelmed, improving responsiveness and availability.

3. Describe high availability.

Answer: High availability (HA) ensures a system remains operational and accessible most of the time, typically through redundancy, failover mechanisms, and load balancing, minimizing downtime.

4. What is the CAP theorem?

Answer: The CAP theorem states that a distributed data store can only guarantee two of the following three properties at any given time:

- Consistency: All nodes see the same data at the same time.

- Availability: Every request receives a response, regardless of the state of any individual node.

- Partition Tolerance: The system continues to operate despite network partitions.

Database Design and Sharding

5. What is database normalization?

Answer: Database normalization is the process of organizing a database to reduce redundancy and improve data integrity by dividing large tables into smaller, related tables.

6. What are the normal forms in database normalization?

Answer: The first three normal forms are:

- 1NF (First Normal Form): Ensures that each column contains atomic values, and each entry in a column is of the same data type.

- 2NF (Second Normal Form): Achieves 1NF and removes partial dependencies on a composite key.

- 3NF (Third Normal Form): Achieves 2NF and removes transitive dependencies.

7. What is sharding?

Answer: Sharding is a database architecture pattern where data is horizontally partitioned across multiple database instances or servers, enabling better performance and scalability.

8. When would you choose sharding over replication?

Answer: Sharding is preferred when the dataset is large and cannot be efficiently handled by a single database instance. It distributes the load across multiple databases, improving performance, whereas replication is used primarily for redundancy and read scaling.

9. What are some challenges associated with sharding?

Answer: Challenges include:

- Complexity of queries: Joining data across shards can be complex and inefficient.

- Data distribution: Uneven data distribution may lead to hot spots, where some shards are overwhelmed while others are underutilized.

- Increased operational overhead: Managing multiple databases requires more maintenance.

Caching Mechanisms (Redis, Memcached)

10. What is caching, and why is it important?

Answer: Caching is the process of storing frequently accessed data in memory for quick retrieval. It reduces latency, improves application performance, and decreases the load on backend systems.

11. Compare Redis and Memcached.

Answer:

- Redis:

- Supports complex data types (strings, hashes, lists, sets).

- Persistence options (snapshotting, AOF).

- Built-in replication and high availability.

- Memcached:

- Simpler key-value store with only string data types.
- Primarily used for caching with no persistence.
- Easier to set up but lacks advanced features.

12. What are cache eviction policies?

Answer: Cache eviction policies determine which data to remove when the cache reaches its capacity. Common policies include:

- Least Recently Used (LRU): Evicts the least recently accessed data.
- First In First Out (FIFO): Evicts the oldest data.
- Least Frequently Used (LFU): Evicts the least frequently accessed data.

13. How do you decide what to cache?

Answer: Cache data that is:

- Frequently accessed and read-heavy.
- Expensive to compute or retrieve.
- Stable, with minimal changes over time to reduce cache invalidation.

API Rate Limiting and Throttling

14. What is API rate limiting?

Answer: API rate limiting restricts the number of requests a user can make to an API within a specified time frame, preventing abuse and ensuring fair usage among users.

15. What are some common strategies for implementing rate limiting?

Answer: Common strategies include:

- Fixed Window: Limits the number of requests in a fixed time period.

- Sliding Window: Counts requests in a moving time frame.

- Token Bucket: Allows bursts of requests but limits the average rate over time.

16. What is throttling?

Answer: Throttling is the process of controlling the amount of traffic sent to a service, often by delaying or queuing requests to ensure the system remains responsive and doesn't exceed its capacity.

17. How do you implement API rate limiting?

Answer: Rate limiting can be implemented using:

- Middleware: Adds rate limiting logic at the application level.

- API Gateway: Implements rate limits across multiple services.

- Redis: Utilizes in-memory storage for tracking request counts and timestamps.

Interview Questions on System Design

18. How would you design a URL shortening service?

Answer: Key components:

- API: Accepts long URLs and generates short URLs.

- Database: Stores mappings of short to long URLs.

- Hashing: Generates unique short codes (e.g., Base62 encoding).

- Redirect Service: Resolves short URLs to long URLs.

19. Describe how you would design a messaging application (like WhatsApp).

Answer: Key features:

- Client-Server Architecture: Clients connect to a central server.

- Message Storage: Use a database to store messages and user data.

- Real-Time Communication: Implement WebSockets for instant messaging.

- Push Notifications: For delivering messages when users are offline.

20. How would you design a system to handle user authentication?

Answer: Components include:

- User Database: Stores user credentials securely (hashed passwords).

- Token Generation: Use JWT (JSON Web Tokens) for stateless authentication.

- OAuth: Integrate with third-party authentication providers.

- Refresh Tokens: Allow users to maintain sessions without re-entering credentials.

21. What considerations would you have for designing a scalable e-commerce platform?

Answer: Consider:

- Microservices Architecture: Separate services for product catalog, order processing, and payment.

- Database Scalability: Use sharding for the product database and replication for read-heavy operations.

- Caching: Implement caching for product data and user sessions.

- Load Balancing: Distribute incoming traffic across multiple instances.

22. How do you approach designing a video streaming service?

Answer: Key elements:

- Content Delivery Network (CDN): Distribute video content globally to reduce latency.

- Transcoding Service: Convert videos into various formats/ resolutions.

- User Management: Store user data and watch history in a scalable database.

- Scalable Architecture: Use microservices for handling different functionalities (upload, playback, recommendation).

23. What metrics would you monitor in a system design?

Answer: Important metrics include:

- Latency: Time taken to process requests.

- Throughput: Number of requests processed per second.

- Error Rates: Percentage of failed requests.

- Resource Utilization: CPU, memory, and disk usage across servers.

24. How do you ensure fault tolerance in a distributed system?

Answer: Implement:

- Redundancy: Duplicate critical components and data.

- Failover Mechanisms: Automatically switch to backup components when failures occur.

- Graceful Degradation: Maintain partial functionality during outages.

25. What is the role of a message queue in system design?

Answer: A message queue enables asynchronous communication between services, allowing them to decouple from each other. It helps manage workload spikes, improves reliability, and ensures messages are processed even if services are down temporarily.

This structured approach to System Design and Architecture provides a comprehensive list of interview questions and concise answers that can guide candidates through preparation for interviews in a Java full stack development context. It covers essential concepts, mechanisms, and practical considerations, offering a solid foundation for further study and discussion.

Chapter 14
Behavioral Interview Preparation

STAR Method for Answering Behavioral Questions

The STAR method is a structured approach to answering behavioral interview questions by discussing the Situation, Task, Action, and Result. This technique helps you provide clear, concise, and compelling responses, making it easier for interviewers to evaluate your experiences and skills.

1. Situation: Describe the context within which you performed a task or faced a challenge. Set the stage for your story.

- Example: "At my previous job, our team was tasked with developing a new feature for our web application, and we had a tight deadline."

2. Task: Explain the specific challenge or responsibility you had in that situation. What was your role?

- Example: "I was responsible for leading the development team, ensuring we met our milestones without compromising on quality."

3. Action: Detail the actions you took to address the task. Focus on your contributions and skills.

- Example: "I organized daily stand-up meetings, assigned tasks based on team strengths, and implemented a code review process to maintain quality."

4. Result: Share the outcomes of your actions. Highlight the impact on the project and any metrics if possible.

- Example: "As a result, we delivered the feature two days ahead of schedule, which increased user engagement by 30%."

Common Behavioral Interview Questions for Developers

1. Tell me about a time you faced a significant challenge at work.

- Answer: "In a previous project, we encountered a major bug just before launch. I quickly coordinated with the team to identify the issue, reallocated resources, and we managed to fix it within hours, ensuring the launch went smoothly."

2. Describe a situation where you had to work under pressure.

- Answer: "During a high-stakes project, our server went down on the day of a major client presentation. I led the team in troubleshooting the issue and implemented a backup solution, allowing us to demo a functional prototype successfully."

3. Can you give an example of a time you had to learn a new technology quickly?

- Answer: "I had to learn React for a project with a tight deadline. I dedicated my evenings to online courses and built a small app to practice. I delivered my first feature in a week, receiving positive feedback from my team."

4. How do you handle constructive criticism?

- Answer: "I view constructive criticism as an opportunity for growth. For instance, after a code review, I received feedback on my code structure. I took the time to understand the suggestions and applied them in future projects, improving my coding standards."

5. Tell me about a time when you had a conflict with a coworker.

- Answer: "I had a disagreement with a teammate about the direction of a project. I suggested we sit down to discuss our viewpoints, which led to a compromise that incorporated both of our ideas and ultimately improved the project outcome."

Handling Teamwork, Conflict, and Leadership Questions

Teamwork Questions

1. Describe a project where you worked as part of a team. What was your role?

- Answer: "I was part of a team developing an e-commerce application. My role involved backend development, collaborating closely with frontend developers to integrate APIs efficiently."

2. How do you approach collaboration with cross-functional teams?

- Answer: "I prioritize open communication and regular updates. For example, in a recent project, I scheduled bi-weekly syncs with marketing and design teams, ensuring everyone was aligned on goals and timelines."

Conflict Resolution Questions

1. Can you give an example of a difficult conversation you had to have with a colleague?

- Answer: "I once had to discuss performance issues with a colleague. I approached the conversation with empathy, focusing on the impact of their work rather than personal attributes, which led to a constructive discussion."

2. How do you deal with team members who are not contributing equally?

- Answer: "I believe in addressing issues directly but tactfully. I would initiate a private conversation to understand their challenges and offer assistance, reinforcing the importance of teamwork."

Leadership Questions

1. What is your leadership style?

- Answer: "My leadership style is participative. I value team input and encourage collaboration. This approach fosters trust and accountability, leading to better outcomes."

2. Describe a time when you had to lead a team through a challenging project.

- Answer: "I led a team during a product launch that faced unexpected delays. I facilitated brainstorming sessions to overcome obstacles, keeping morale high and ensuring that we successfully launched the product on the rescheduled date."

Time Management and Problem-Solving Skills

Time Management Questions

1. How do you prioritize tasks in a project?

- Answer: "I use a combination of urgency and importance. For instance, I categorize tasks using the Eisenhower Matrix, allowing me to focus on critical tasks while delegating or scheduling less urgent ones."

2. Tell me about a time when you missed a deadline. What happened?

- Answer: "I once underestimated the complexity of a feature and missed the deadline. I immediately communicated with my manager, adjusted the timeline, and worked overtime to complete it, ensuring I learned to assess project scopes more accurately in the future."

Problem-Solving Questions

1. Describe a complex problem you solved. What was your approach?

- Answer: "Our application was experiencing performance issues. I analyzed logs and pinpointed database queries as the bottleneck. I optimized the queries and implemented caching, resulting in a 50% decrease in load time."

2. How do you approach troubleshooting a technical issue?

- Answer: "I follow a systematic approach: I first replicate the issue, check logs for errors, and consult documentation. If needed, I reach out to team members for insights. This methodical approach often leads to quick resolutions."

Additional Behavioral Questions for Preparation

1. Have you ever taken the initiative to improve a process?

- Answer: "I noticed our deployment process was manual and prone to errors. I researched CI/CD tools, implemented a pipeline using Jenkins, and reduced deployment time by 75%."

2. How do you balance multiple projects with competing deadlines?

- Answer: "I assess each project's requirements and deadlines, then create a detailed schedule. I also communicate regularly with stakeholders to manage expectations and reprioritize as necessary."

3. Tell me about a time you received negative feedback. How did you handle it?

- Answer: "I received feedback on my communication style during team meetings. I took it to heart, asked for specific examples, and worked on being more concise and open to others' ideas, which improved team dynamics."

4. Describe a time when you had to adapt to significant changes at work.

- Answer: "When our team transitioned to remote work, I adapted by setting up virtual communication tools and encouraging regular check-ins. This fostered collaboration and kept the team connected."

5. What do you consider your biggest professional achievement?

- Answer: "My biggest achievement was leading a project that increased user engagement by over 40%. I utilized analytics to identify user pain points and implemented changes that greatly improved the user experience."

Conclusion

Preparing for behavioral interview questions is crucial for showcasing your skills and experiences effectively. By using the STAR method, practicing common questions, and focusing on your teamwork, conflict resolution, leadership, time management, and problem-solving skills, you can present yourself as a strong candidate. Reflecting on your past experiences and articulating them clearly will help you stand out in the competitive job market for Java Full Stack Developers.

This section provides an overview of key behavioral interview techniques and questions that Java Full Stack Developers might encounter, emphasizing clear and concise responses to demonstrate relevant skills and experiences.

Chapter 15
Mock Interviews and Coding Challenges

What to Expect in a Technical Interview

1. What are the typical stages of a technical interview?

Answer: A technical interview usually consists of multiple stages: an initial phone screen, technical assessment (coding test), in-person interviews (often including system design), and behavioral interviews.

2. What types of questions are asked in a technical interview?

Answer: Questions can be categorized into coding problems, system design, algorithms, data structures, databases, and domain-specific queries.

3. How long do technical interviews usually last?

Answer: Most technical interviews last between 30 to 90 minutes, depending on the role and company.

4. How should I prepare for a technical interview?

Answer: Review key concepts in algorithms, data structures, system design, and practice coding problems on platforms like LeetCode or HackerRank.

5. What is the importance of the STAR method in interviews?

Answer: The STAR method (Situation, Task, Action, Result) helps structure answers to behavioral questions, showcasing problem-solving and critical thinking skills.

How to Approach Coding Challenges (Problem-Solving Techniques)

1. What is the first step when faced with a coding problem?

Answer: Read the problem statement carefully and clarify any ambiguities before starting to code.

2. How should I break down the problem?

Answer: Divide the problem into smaller parts or steps, and understand the requirements and constraints for each part.

3. Why is it important to discuss my thought process aloud?

Answer: Verbalizing your thought process helps the interviewer understand your approach, logic, and problem-solving skills.

4. What is a good strategy for writing code during an interview?

Answer: Write clean, modular code with proper naming conventions and include comments to explain your logic.

5. How do I handle unexpected challenges during coding?

Answer: Stay calm, think logically, and if you encounter a block, re-evaluate your approach or consider alternative solutions.

Mock Interview Examples and Role-Play

1. How can I simulate a mock interview?

Answer: Partner with a peer or use online platforms like Pramp or Interviewing.io to conduct mock interviews.

2. What types of questions should I practice in a mock interview?

Answer: Focus on common coding questions, system design problems, and behavioral questions relevant to the role.

3. How should I evaluate my performance in a mock interview?

Answer: Reflect on areas of strength and weakness, and seek feedback from your interviewer on your technical and communication skills.

4. What is an example of a coding question for practice?

Example: "Given a list of integers, write a function to return the two numbers that add up to a specific target."

5. What are some common system design questions?

Example: "Design a URL shortening service like bit.ly" or "How would you design a ride-sharing app?"

Preparing for Whiteboard or Live Coding Interviews

1. How should I prepare for whiteboard interviews?

Answer: Practice coding by hand, focusing on clarity of thought and organization since you'll have no IDE to help.

2. What are some tips for writing code on a whiteboard?

Answer: Write legibly, use proper indentation, and explain your thought process as you write to engage the interviewer.

3. What is the importance of edge cases in whiteboard coding?

Answer: Discussing edge cases demonstrates thoroughness and helps ensure your solution is robust and handles unexpected inputs.

4. How should I structure my code on a whiteboard?

Answer: Use a clear and consistent format: define the function first, outline inputs/outputs, and then implement the logic step by step.

5. How do I handle mistakes made while coding on a whiteboard?

Answer: Acknowledge the mistake, explain how you would fix it, and make corrections as needed without panicking.

Resources for Practicing Coding Challenges

1. What are some popular coding challenge platforms?

Answer: LeetCode, HackerRank, CodeSignal, and Codewars are excellent resources for practicing coding problems.

2. How can I use LeetCode effectively?

Answer: Focus on problems categorized by difficulty, practice frequently asked interview questions, and review solutions for different approaches.

3. Are there books that can help with coding interviews?

Answer: "Cracking the Coding Interview" by Gayle Laakmann McDowell and "Elements of Programming Interviews" by Adnan Aziz are highly recommended.

4. What is the benefit of using mock interview platforms?

Answer: Mock interview platforms provide real-time feedback and simulate the interview experience, helping candidates feel more comfortable.

5. How important is it to practice behavioral interview questions?

Answer: Practicing behavioral questions is crucial, as they assess cultural fit, teamwork, and problem-solving abilities in real-world scenarios.

This condensed chapter captures key points, questions, and answers that aspiring Java Full Stack developers can use as a reference for preparing for mock interviews and coding challenges. Each section can be expanded with additional detail, examples, or explanations as needed.

Chapter 16
Problem Solving: Coding Practice

This involve covering a wide range of topics from basic algorithms to complex data structures, object-oriented programming, and practical web-based problems. Here is a structured approach to break down and summarize key areas.

1. Basic Problem-Solving with Arrays and Strings

Problem 1: Reverse a String

- Description: Write a Java program to reverse a given string without using additional space.

- Input: "hello"

- Output: "olleh"

- Approach:

- Convert the string into a character array.

- Use two-pointer technique, one starting from the beginning and the other from the end, and swap characters until the middle is reached.

Problem 2: Find the Missing Number in an Array

- Description: Given an array of integers of size `n`, where the numbers are in the range from 1 to `n+1` with one number missing, find the missing number.

- Input: [1, 2, 4, 5, 6]

- Output: 3

- Approach:

- Use the formula for the sum of the first `n` numbers: `Sum = n(n+1)/2`.

- Subtract the sum of the array from this total to find the missing number.

Problem 3: Find the First Non-Repeated Character

- Description: Given a string, find the first character that does not repeat.

- Input: "swiss"

- Output: "w"

- Approach:

- Use a HashMap to store the frequency of each character.

- Traverse the string a second time to check for the first character with a count of 1.

Problem 4: Maximum Subarray Sum (Kadane's Algorithm)

- Description: Given an array of integers, find the contiguous subarray with the largest sum.

- Input: [-2, 1, -3, 4, -1, 2, 1, -5, 4]

- Output: 6 (subarray: [4, -1, 2, 1])

- Approach:

- Use Kadane's algorithm: maintain a current sum and update a global maximum sum whenever a larger sum is found.

2. Sorting and Searching

Problem 5: Merge Two Sorted Arrays

- Description: Given two sorted arrays, merge them into a single sorted array.

- Input: [1, 3, 5], [2, 4, 6]

- Output: [1, 2, 3, 4, 5, 6]

- Approach:

- Use two pointers, one for each array. Compare elements and append the smaller one to the result array until both arrays are exhausted.

Problem 6: Find the Median of Two Sorted Arrays

- Description: Given two sorted arrays, find their median in $O(\log(\min(n, m)))$ time complexity.

- Input: [1, 3], [2]

- Output: 2.0

- Approach:

- Apply binary search on the smaller array to partition both arrays in such a way that the elements on the left side of the partition are smaller than the elements on the right.

Problem 7: Quick Sort Implementation

- Description: Implement the QuickSort algorithm to sort an array of integers.

- Input: [3, 6, 8, 10, 1, 2, 1]

- Output: [1, 1, 2, 3, 6, 8, 10]

- Approach:

- Select a pivot, partition the array into two halves, and recursively apply the same process to each half.

Problem 8: Binary Search on a Rotated Sorted Array

- Description: Given a rotated sorted array, find an element using binary search in O(log n) time.

- Input: [4, 5, 6, 7, 0, 1, 2], target = 0

- Output: 4 (index of 0)

- Approach:

- Check the middle element; if the left half is sorted, the target must be in the sorted half or else search the other half. Apply binary search iteratively.

3. Dynamic Programming

Problem 9: Longest Common Subsequence (LCS)

- Description: Find the length of the longest common subsequence between two strings.

- Input: "AGGTAB", "GXTXAYB"

- Output: 4 (The longest common subsequence is "GTAB")

- Approach:

- Use dynamic programming with a 2D table to store the lengths of common subsequences.

Problem 10: Coin Change Problem

- Description: Given a set of coin denominations and a target amount, find the minimum number of coins that make up the amount.

- Input: $[1, 2, 5]$, amount $= 11$

- Output: 3 (11 can be made with $[5, 5, 1]$)

- Approach:

- Use a dynamic programming table where `dp[i]` represents the minimum coins needed for amount `i`.

Problem 11: 0/1 Knapsack Problem

- Description: Given weights and values of items, find the maximum value that can be carried in a knapsack of a given capacity.

- Input: weights $= [1, 3, 4, 5]$, values $= [1, 4, 5, 7]$, capacity $= 7$

- Output: 9

- Approach:

- Build a DP table where the value at each cell `dp[i][j]` represents the maximum value with the first `i` items and capacity `j`.

4. Graph Algorithms

Problem 12: Depth-First Search (DFS)

- Description: Implement Depth-First Search for a graph and print the nodes in DFS order.

- Input: Graph represented as adjacency list

- Output: Nodes in DFS order

- Approach:

- Use a stack or recursion to visit each node, marking them as visited to avoid cycles.

Problem 13: Dijkstra's Algorithm

- Description: Implement Dijkstra's algorithm to find the shortest path from a source to all other vertices in a graph.

- Input: Weighted graph and source node

- Output: Shortest distance to all nodes

- Approach:

- Use a priority queue to explore nodes in increasing order of distance, updating the shortest paths as you go.

Problem 14: Detect a Cycle in a Graph

- Description: Write a program to detect if there is a cycle in an undirected graph.
    - Input: Graph represented as an adjacency list
    - Output: True or False (whether a cycle exists)
    - Approach:
    - Use DFS and check if any visited node is revisited before completing the traversal.

5. Object-Oriented Programming

Problem 15: Design a Parking Lot System

- Description: Design a system for managing a parking lot that includes tracking available spaces, managing check-ins, and payments.
    - Classes: `ParkingLot`, `ParkingSpace`, `Vehicle`, `Ticket`
    - Approach:
    - Use classes to represent different entities. Methods include checking for available spaces, assigning spaces, and calculating parking fees.

Problem 16: Design a Movie Ticket Booking System

- Description: Design an online movie ticket booking system that manages seat reservations, cancellations, and movie show timings.
    - Classes: `Theater`, `Show`, `Seat`, `Booking`
    - Approach:
    - Create class hierarchies, use data structures to represent seat availability, and manage reservations through object interactions.

6. Concurrency and Multithreading

Problem 17: Producer-Consumer Problem

- Description: Implement the producer-consumer problem using threads in Java, where one thread produces data and the other consumes it.
    - Input: n/a
    - Output: Correctly synchronized production and consumption of items.
    - Approach:

- Use Java's `wait()` and `notify()` methods to manage synchronization between threads.

Problem 18: Implement Singleton Design Pattern

- Description: Write a thread-safe implementation of the Singleton design pattern.

- Approach:

- Use the `synchronized` keyword to ensure that only one instance of the class is created across multiple threads.

7. Miscellaneous

Problem 19: Valid Parentheses

- Description: Given a string containing parentheses, check if the parentheses are valid (well-formed).

- Input: "(())"

- Output: True

- Approach:

- Use a stack to track opening and closing parentheses.

Problem 20: LRU Cache Implementation

- Description: Implement an LRU (Least Recently Used) cache with get and put operations.

- Input: n/a

- Output: Correct cache operations.

- Approach:

- Use a LinkedHashMap or a combination of a Doubly Linked List and a HashMap to ensure $O(1)$ access and insertion times.

These problems cover a broad range of essential topics for Java full-stack developers, from algorithmic problem-solving to real-world system designs and concurrency, making it a comprehensive preparation tool for interviews or technical evaluations.

Chapter 17
Top 90 Commonly Asked Questions

Java Basics and Object-Oriented Programming (OOP)

1. Write a program to reverse a string in Java without using in-built methods.

2. Explain how to implement a Singleton design pattern in Java.

3. Demonstrate method overloading and method overriding in Java.

4. What is the difference between `==` and `equals()` in Java?

5. Write a program to find the second-largest number in an array.

6. Explain how `HashMap` works internally in Java.

7. How does garbage collection work in Java?

8. Write a Java program to check if a number is prime.

9. What is the difference between `ArrayList` and `LinkedList` in Java?

10. Implement a custom `Comparator` to sort objects by multiple fields.

Algorithms and Problem Solving

11. Write a Java program to check if a string is a palindrome.

12. Explain and implement the Merge Sort algorithm.

13. How do you find the intersection of two arrays in Java?

14. Write a program to find the missing number in an array of size `n`.

15. Find the longest increasing subsequence in an array.

16. Implement the binary search algorithm in Java.

17. How would you detect and resolve a cycle in a linked list?

18. Write a program to sort an array using Quick Sort.

19. Solve the "Two Sum" problem using Java.

20. Find the maximum sum subarray using Kadane's Algorithm.

Data Structures

21. Explain how to implement a stack using an array and linked list.

22. Write a program to reverse a linked list.

23. How would you implement a queue using two stacks?

24. Write a program to merge two sorted linked lists.

25. Find the kth largest element in an unsorted array.

26. Implement a binary tree and write a function to perform an in-order traversal.

27. How do you check if two binary trees are identical?

28. Write a Java program to find the height of a binary tree.

29. What is a heap data structure? Implement a max heap in Java.

30. Explain how a balanced binary search tree works and implement an AVL tree.

Concurrency and Multithreading

31. What is the difference between `synchronized` and `volatile` in Java?

32. Write a Java program that demonstrates thread synchronization.

33. How do you implement the producer-consumer problem using threads in Java?

34. What are `Callable` and `Future` in Java? How are they different from `Runnable`?

35. Write a program to create a deadlock in Java and explain how to avoid it.

36. How does the `ThreadPoolExecutor` work in Java?

37. Explain the difference between `wait()`, `notify()`, and `notifyAll()`.

38. What is the difference between `Executor` and `ExecutorService`?

Spring Framework (Backend)

39. What is Dependency Injection and how is it implemented in Spring?

40. Explain the difference between `@Controller`, `@RestController`, and `@Service` annotations in Spring.

41. How do you handle exceptions in Spring Boot applications?

42. What is Spring Boot's `@Autowired` annotation and how does it work?

43. Write a basic CRUD application using Spring Boot and JPA.

44. How do you secure a Spring Boot application using Spring Security?

45. What is the difference between `@Transactional` and `@RequestMapping` in Spring?

46. How does Spring Boot auto-configuration work?

47. Explain Spring Boot's actuator and its use cases.

48. How do you implement pagination in a Spring Boot REST API?

49. What is the `@PathVariable` and `@RequestParam` annotation in Spring Boot?

50. How do you integrate Spring Boot with a MySQL database?
Database (SQL/NoSQL)

51. Write an SQL query to find the nth highest salary in a table.

52. Explain how you would optimize a query that joins large tables.

53. What are ACID properties in a database and why are they important?

54. How do you perform a left join and right join in SQL?

55. Write a query to find duplicate records in a table.

56. What is database indexing? How does it improve performance?

57. How do you implement transactions in Spring Boot with JPA?

58. What is a NoSQL database, and when would you choose MongoDB over a relational database?

59. Write a query to group data by a specific column and calculate the average.

60. Explain normalization and its levels in database design.

Front-End (JavaScript, Angular, React)

61. Explain the difference between `var`, `let`, and `const` in JavaScript.

62. What is the Document Object Model (DOM) and how does it work?

63. How does Angular's two-way data binding work?

64. Explain the component lifecycle in React and its hooks (e.g., `useEffect`).

65. What is the purpose of state management in front-end frameworks like React or Angular?

66. How do you handle form validation in Angular or React?

67. Explain how you can implement routing in a React application.

68. What is the role of TypeScript in Angular?

69. How does the virtual DOM improve performance in React?

70. Explain how to implement lazy loading in Angular/React.

Microservices and Cloud Technologies

71. What are microservices and how do they differ from monolithic architecture?

72. How do you use Spring Cloud for microservices?

73. Explain the role of Eureka in service discovery in Spring Cloud.

74. How do you implement load balancing in a microservice architecture?

75. Explain how Docker can be used in the deployment of Java applications.

76. What is Kubernetes, and how does it help in container orchestration?

77. How do you handle communication between microservices?

78. What are the advantages and challenges of using RESTful APIs in microservices?

79. How do you implement API Gateway using Spring Cloud?

80. How do you handle security in a microservice-based architecture?

Miscellaneous/Advanced Concepts

81. What is the `Optional` class in Java 8 and how does it help in avoiding null pointer exceptions?

82. Explain how the `Stream` API works in Java 8 and give an example of its use.

83. What is a lambda expression in Java and how does it simplify code?

84. How does the `CompletableFuture` class in Java 8 help in asynchronous programming?

85. What is the difference between SOAP and REST web services?

86. How do you design a scalable system that can handle millions of users?

87. Explain the CAP theorem in distributed computing.

88. How do you optimize the performance of a Java-based web application?

89. What is the difference between vertical scaling and horizontal scaling?

90. What is Circuit Breaker Pattern in microservices and how do you implement it in Spring Boot?

Chapter 18
Top Java Stream: Mostly Asked

The examples provide practical use cases with stream logic code snippets.

1. Filtering a List

Question: Filter a list of integers to find even numbers.

java

Solution:

```java
List<Integer> numbers = Arrays.asList(1, 2, 3, 4, 5, 6);
List<Integer> evenNumbers = numbers.stream()
.filter(n -> n % 2 == 0)
.collect(Collectors.toList());
```

2. Mapping Values

Question: Convert a list of strings to their lengths.

java

Solution:

```java
List<String> names = Arrays.asList("Alice", "Bob", "Charlie");
List<Integer> nameLengths = names.stream()
.map(String::length)
.collect(Collectors.toList());
```

3. Finding Maximum

Question: Find the maximum value in a list of integers.

java

Solution:

```java
List<Integer> numbers = Arrays.asList(1, 3, 5, 7, 2, 4);
Optional<Integer> maxNumber = numbers.stream()
```

```java
.max(Integer::compare);
```

4. Finding Minimum

Question: Find the minimum value in a list of integers.

```java
java
Solution:
List<Integer> numbers = Arrays.asList(1, 3, 5, 7, 2, 4);
Optional<Integer> minNumber = numbers.stream()
.min(Integer::compare);
```

5. Counting Elements

Question: Count the number of elements in a list that are greater than 5.

```java
java
Solution:
List<Integer> numbers = Arrays.asList(1, 3, 5, 7, 9, 2);
long count = numbers.stream()
.filter(n -> n > 5)
.count();
```

6. Summing Values

Question: Calculate the sum of all integers in a list.

```java
java
Solution:
List<Integer> numbers = Arrays.asList(1, 2, 3, 4, 5);
int sum = numbers.stream()
.mapToInt(Integer::intValue)
.sum();
```

7. Average Calculation

Question: Find the average of a list of integers.

java
Solution:
```java
List<Integer> numbers = Arrays.asList(1, 2, 3, 4, 5);
OptionalDouble average = numbers.stream()
.mapToInt(Integer::intValue)
.average();
```

8. Distinct Elements

Question: Get distinct elements from a list of integers.

java
Solution:
```java
List<Integer> numbers = Arrays.asList(1, 2, 2, 3, 4, 4, 5);
List<Integer> distinctNumbers = numbers.stream()
.distinct()
.collect(Collectors.toList());
```

9. Sorting a List

Question: Sort a list of strings in alphabetical order.

java
Solution:
```java
List<String> names = Arrays.asList("Charlie", "Alice", "Bob");
List<String> sortedNames = names.stream()
.sorted()
.collect(Collectors.toList());
```

10. Reversing a List

Question: Reverse a list of integers.

java
Solution:
```java
List<Integer> numbers = Arrays.asList(1, 2, 3, 4, 5);
List<Integer> reversedNumbers = numbers.stream()
```

```java
.sorted(Comparator.reverseOrder())
.collect(Collectors.toList());
```

11. Joining Strings

Question: Join a list of strings into a single string with commas.

java

Solution:

```java
List<String> names = Arrays.asList("Alice", "Bob", "Charlie");
String joinedNames = names.stream()
.collect(Collectors.joining(", "));
```

12. Partitioning Elements

Question: Partition a list of integers into even and odd numbers.

java

Solution:

```java
List<Integer> numbers = Arrays.asList(1, 2, 3, 4, 5);
Map<Boolean, List<Integer>> partitioned = numbers.stream()
.collect(Collectors.partitioningBy(n -> n % 2 == 0));
```

13. Grouping Elements

Question: Group a list of strings by their length.

java

Solution:

```java
List<String> names = Arrays.asList("Alice", "Bob", "Charlie", "David");
Map<Integer, List<String>> groupedByLength = names.stream()
.collect(Collectors.groupingBy(String::length));
```

14. Finding First Match

Question: Find the first string that starts with "A".

java

Solution:

```java
List<String> names = Arrays.asList("Charlie", "Bob", "Alice", "David");
Optional<String> firstA = names.stream()
.filter(name -> name.startsWith("A"))
.findFirst();
```

15. Flattening a List of Lists

Question: Flatten a list of lists of integers into a single list.

java

Solution:

```java
List<List<Integer>> listOfLists = Arrays.asList(Arrays.asList(1, 2), Arrays.asList(3, 4));
List<Integer> flatList = listOfLists.stream()
.flatMap(List::stream)
.collect(Collectors.toList());
```

16. Creating a Map

Question: Create a map from a list of strings where the key is the string and the value is its length.

java

Solution:

```java
List<String> names = Arrays.asList("Alice", "Bob", "Charlie");
Map<String, Integer> nameMap = names.stream()
.collect(Collectors.toMap(name -> name, String::length));
```

17. Finding Duplicates

Question: Find duplicates in a list of integers.

java

Solution:

```java
List<Integer> numbers = Arrays.asList(1, 2, 3, 2, 3, 4, 5);
```

```java
Set<Integer> duplicates = numbers.stream()
.filter(i -> Collections.frequency(numbers, i) > 1)
.collect(Collectors.toSet());
```

18. Extracting Unique Characters

Question: Extract unique characters from a string.

java

Solution:

```java
String str = "Hello World";
Set<Character> uniqueChars = str.chars()
.mapToObj(c -> (char) c)
.collect(Collectors.toSet());
```

19. Counting Frequency of Elements

Question: Count the frequency of each element in a list.

java

Solution:

```java
List<String> names = Arrays.asList("Alice", "Bob", "Alice", "Charlie", "Bob");
Map<String, Long> frequencyMap = names.stream()
.collect(Collectors.groupingBy(name -> name, Collectors.counting()));
```

20. Calculating Factorials

Question: Calculate the factorial of numbers from 1 to 5.

java

Solution:

```java
List<Integer> numbers = Arrays.asList(1, 2, 3, 4, 5);
List<Integer> factorials = numbers.stream()
.map(n -> IntStream.rangeClosed(1, n).reduce(1, (a, b) -> a * b))
.collect(Collectors.toList());
```

21. Merging Two Lists

Question: Merge two lists of integers and remove duplicates.

java

Solution:

```java
List<Integer> list1 = Arrays.asList(1, 2, 3);
List<Integer> list2 = Arrays.asList(3, 4, 5);
List<Integer> mergedList = Stream.concat(list1.stream(), list2.stream())
    .distinct()
    .collect(Collectors.toList());
```

22. Finding Palindromes

Question: Find all palindromic strings from a list.

java

Solution:

```java
List<String> words = Arrays.asList("madam", "racecar", "hello", "world");
List<String> palindromes = words.stream()
    .filter(word -> new StringBuilder(word).reverse().toString().equals(word))
    .collect(Collectors.toList());
```

23. Calculating Powers

Question: Calculate squares of numbers from 1 to 5.

java

Solution:

```java
List<Integer> numbers = Arrays.asList(1, 2, 3, 4, 5);
List<Integer> squares = numbers.stream()
    .map(n -> n * n)
    .collect(Collectors.toList());
```

24. Finding Common Elements

Question: Find common elements between two lists.

```java
Solution:
List<Integer> list1 = Arrays.asList(1, 2, 3, 4);
List<Integer> list2 = Arrays.asList(3, 4, 5, 6);
List<Integer> commonElements = list1.stream()
.filter(list2::contains)
.collect(Collectors.toList());
```

25. Transforming a List of Objects

Question: Convert a list of objects to a list of a specific property (e.g., names).

```java
Solution:
class Person {
String name;
// Constructor, getters, setters
}
List<Person> people = Arrays.asList(new Person("Alice"), new Person("Bob"), new Person("Charlie"));
List<String> names = people.stream()
.map(Person::getName)
.collect(Collectors.toList());
```

26. Calculating Cumulative Sum

Question: Calculate the cumulative sum of a list of integers.

```java
Solution:
List<Integer> numbers = Arrays.asList(1, 2, 3, 4);
List<Integer> cumulativeSum = new ArrayList<>();
```

```java
AtomicInteger sum = new AtomicInteger(0);
numbers.forEach(n
```

Chapter 19
Final Interview Day: Tips for Success

How to Prepare the Day Before

1. Review Your Materials:

- Go over your resume and the job description again to ensure you understand what the employer is looking for.

- Prepare a list of potential questions and answers, especially those related to your experiences and skills.

2. Research the Company:

- Familiarize yourself with the company's products, services, and culture. Review recent news articles or press releases.

- Understand the company's mission and values to tailor your responses to align with their goals.

3. Plan Your Outfit:

- Choose a professional outfit that suits the company culture. Lay it out the night before to avoid any last-minute decisions.

4. Prepare Your Documents:

- Print multiple copies of your resume, cover letter, and any relevant work samples.

- Bring a notebook and pen for taking notes during the interview.

5. Practice Common Interview Questions:

- Use the STAR method (Situation, Task, Action, Result) to structure your responses to behavioral questions.

- Conduct a mock interview with a friend or family member to practice articulating your thoughts clearly.

6. Plan Your Journey:

- Confirm the time and location of your interview. If it's in person, check the best route to the venue.

- Allow extra time for unforeseen delays, and consider making a trial run if possible.

7. Get a Good Night's Sleep:

- Aim for 7-8 hours of sleep to ensure you are well-rested and alert on the interview day.

- Avoid stimulants like caffeine in excess that may disrupt your sleep.

Managing Interview Anxiety

1. Practice Deep Breathing:

- Take deep, slow breaths to calm your nerves. Inhale for a count of four, hold for four, and exhale for four.

- Repeat this several times before entering the interview room to reduce anxiety.

2. Visualize Success:

- Spend a few minutes visualizing a successful interview. Picture yourself answering questions confidently and engaging with the interviewers.

3. Shift Your Focus:

- Concentrate on the opportunity rather than the pressure of the interview. Think of it as a conversation to learn more about the company and role.

4. Prepare for the Worst:

- Acknowledge that it's okay to not have all the answers. Prepare for questions you might find challenging by thinking through how you would handle them.

- If you don't know an answer, it's acceptable to express your thought process rather than panicking.

5. Stay Positive:

- Remind yourself of your skills and qualifications. Focus on what you bring to the table.

- Use positive affirmations like "I am capable" or "I can handle this" to boost your confidence.

6. Engage in Physical Activity:

- Engage in light exercise or stretching before the interview to release tension and boost endorphins.

- Consider going for a walk to clear your mind.

Negotiating Salary and Benefits Post-Interview

1. Do Your Research:

- Research industry salary standards for the position using websites like Glassdoor, Payscale, or LinkedIn Salary Insights.

- Consider factors like your experience, the company's size, and location when determining your desired salary range.

2. Wait for the Right Moment:

- Allow the employer to bring up the salary discussion. Usually, it's best to discuss compensation after receiving a job offer.

3. Express Enthusiasm:

- When discussing salary, express your enthusiasm for the position. You can say, "I'm really excited about the opportunity to contribute to the team and grow my skills here."

4. Be Flexible:

- Be open to negotiation on benefits beyond salary, such as remote work options, flexible hours, additional vacation days, or professional development opportunities.

5. Communicate Clearly:

- When presenting your salary expectations, communicate clearly and confidently. For example, "Based on my research and experience, I was hoping for a salary in the range of $X to $Y."

6. Consider Total Compensation:

- Evaluate the complete compensation package, including bonuses, health benefits, retirement plans, and stock options.

- Sometimes, non-monetary benefits can significantly enhance overall job satisfaction.

7. Be Professional:

- Regardless of the outcome, maintain professionalism. If the offer doesn't meet your expectations, thank them for the offer and express your interest in finding a middle ground.

Dos and Don'ts During the Interview

Dos:

1. Dress Appropriately:

- Wear professional attire that aligns with the company culture, even if the environment is casual.

2. Be Punctual:

- Arrive at the interview location 10-15 minutes early to show respect for the interviewer's time.

3. Maintain Eye Contact:

- Engage with your interviewers by maintaining eye contact, which conveys confidence and interest.

4. Listen Actively:

- Listen carefully to the questions being asked and take a moment to formulate your responses.

5. Ask Thoughtful Questions:

- Prepare insightful questions about the company, team dynamics, or future projects to demonstrate your interest.

6. Follow Up:

- Send a thank-you email within 24 hours to express your appreciation for the opportunity and reiterate your interest in the position.

Don'ts:

1. Don't Speak Negatively:

- Avoid disparaging previous employers or colleagues; this can raise red flags about your attitude.

2. Don't Fidget:

- Avoid distracting body language, like fidgeting or crossing your arms. Sit up straight and maintain a relaxed posture.

3. Don't Interrupt:

- Allow the interviewer to finish speaking before you respond. Interrupting can come across as rude.

4. Don't Be Overly Casual:

- Keep the tone professional and avoid slang or overly familiar language.

5. Don't Memorize Answers:

- Instead of memorizing responses, focus on understanding key points you want to communicate. This will make your answers sound more natural.

6. Don't Rush Your Answers:

- Take your time to think about your responses. A brief pause is acceptable if you need to gather your thoughts.

7. Don't Forget to Smile:

- A genuine smile can create a positive atmosphere and help you connect with the interviewers.

The final interview day is your chance to shine. By preparing effectively, managing anxiety, and navigating salary discussions skillfully, you can create a strong impression. Remember to be yourself, communicate your passion for the role, and stay professional throughout the process. Good luck!

This concise chapter provides clear, actionable advice while addressing key areas that candidates often find crucial on interview day. Adjustments can be made based on specific audiences or additional insights you'd like to include!